The Golden Age of EASY LISTENING

Derek Taylor

sonicbondpublishing.com

Sonicbond Publishing Limited
www.sonicbondpublishing.co.uk
Email: info@sonicbondpublishing.co.uk

First Published in the United Kingdom 2023
First Published in the United States 2023

British Library Cataloguing in Publication Data:
A Catalogue record for this book is available from the British Library

ISBN 978-1-78952-285-3

Typeset in ITC Garamond & ITC Avant Garde
Printed and bound in England

Graphic design and typesetting: Full Moon Media

The Golden Age of EASY LISTENING

Derek Taylor

sonicbondpublishing.com

Dedication

For Stuart Bowman

Acknowledgements

I'd like to thank my IT mentor, Adam Farnes, for help in compiling the various discographies and for researching photographs and images; Darren Nicholas for his help in understanding and describing the musical arrangements of the artists; Mr Cool, John Champneys, for sharing the cosiness of his farmhouse kitchen; and my brother Roy for his enthusiasm and useful knowledge of blues and jazz guitar. Above all, I'd like to thank my much-treasured Pat for putting up with my absences during the long hours of research and writing.

Additionally, I'd like to thank Stephen Lambe for commissioning this work, and my editor Dominic Sanderson for his wise and invaluable guidance.

The Golden Age of EASY LISTENING

Contents

Introduction

A musical potpourri, easy listening music induces in its listeners a romantic state of mind by bringing together the simple and catchy melodies of smooth pop and dance hits, along with original compositions, and arranging them around a heavenly, otherworldly even, mixture of orchestral instrumentations and choral wordless vocalisations. As such, it can hardly be called a musical genre, but more a spell cast over its listeners.

I first came under the spell of this wonderful music as a young boy going to the cinema on Saturday mornings around 1961. I am talking in this book, particularly about orchestral and instrumental music. In those days, before most families possessed a television set, cinemas would put on Saturday morning matinee shows just for the kids. They'd show a 'B' Movie cowboy film series featuring the likes of Gene Autry and Roy Rogers, which we kids loved. Cinemas were the only places you could get such entertainment in those days, and Saturday morning matinees were about the only times kids could go to the cinema on their own. It didn't cost much to get in and the cinemas would be packed with kids from all over town and beyond. Easy listening music was played before the show started while the audience filed in to take their seats and while they waited for the film to begin. It was played again in the intervals between films when refreshments were on sale. Most kids were oblivious to this background music as they chatted with their friends and ate their ice creams and drank their 'pop' (fizzy drinks of varying types and brands). But somehow, it caught my attention. Above all the din and the fun and mischief-making going on all around me, the music somehow got to me. I heard it and I loved it. I didn't know what I was hearing; I just loved it. They were beautiful, catchy tunes full of a magical kind of sweetness that swept me along on their waves of soaring violins, tinkling pianos and the whole gambit of orchestral instruments arranged in such a way as to, as I later came to realise, 'heal the heart's mood of every man…'. The quotation at the end of the last sentence comes from an Anglo-Saxon poem that is, in fact, talking about words and books. But, as I got older and began to hear easy listening music in all manner of public places and on the BBC Home Service – which later became pop station Radio 2, where you will never now hear it played – I came to realise that these words could be applied just as meaningfully to music, and particularly easy listening music.

As a boy, apart from piling into the cinema with my five brothers – I was a twin in the middle – I mostly just wanted to stay at home and be with my mother (my father, a soldier, was often away on overseas postings). Mother, a refugee from the war in Burma in WW2, had trekked through the jungle to India to escape the Japanese, nearly dying on the way from starvation, typhoid and dysentery. She survived, but practically all her family died on that journey from hell. As a result, she bottled up – in the days before post-traumatic stress disorder was understood, let alone diagnosed – a lot of unexpressed misery. The war, for those who endured the cruelty of it first-hand, was something her generation rarely, if ever, spoke about. But I could feel it in her and sensed that one of the few things that soothed her was music and, particularly, the sweet arrangements of the 'simple and catchy melodies' of what was called 'mood music' before it came to be called easy listening music. I could see it 'healing the [her] heart's mood…' as the Anglo-Saxon poet said 'words' could.

It wasn't long before I began to hear the names of the band leaders and their orchestras whose recordings my mother and I were listening to: Mantovani, Percy Faith, Acker Bilk, Ray Conniff, Billy Vaughn, Norrie Paramour, Lawrence Welk, Floyd Cramer, Ron Goodwin, Bert Kaempfert, Bert Weedon, Les Baxter, Martin Denny, Henry Mancini, James Last and so many more as the next few years rolled on by. Their names meant wonderful things to me, just as the names of groups like The Beatles, The Rolling Stones, The Beach Boys and the Hollies began to mean to my generation just a few years later. I turned on to the pop music of the day in a big way as I grew into adolescence and adulthood, but always calling me back whenever I heard it in department stores, cinemas, hotels and all manner of public places were the seductively pleasant sounds of my easy listening musical heroes. And then those heroes began to cover the pop songs I loved almost as much. Wow! And I was hooked all over again. Radio Caroline took over the airwaves, but for a while, the BBC Home Service continued for what remained of the 1960s to fill the airwaves with the old easy listening orchestras and soon a new generation of easy listening band leaders. I could have the best of both worlds! If I'd lived in America, I'd have had my pick of an explosion of FM easy listening stations playing what was newly labelled 'the beautiful music', but alas, I did not. I lived in Britain, a country where the BBC and government, for their own paternalistic reasons, diligently guarded the granting of radio licences. Nevertheless, there were still the records and delightful evenings in with my mother, not forgetting the music played during the day when BBC TV's new station, BBC 2, was not broadcasting 24-hour-a-day programming. What you got instead was music played to a still 'test card' image giving the channel's ID.

Easy listening music now takes all sorts of forms, most of it sung by lead vocalists, from Muzak to MOR (Middle of the Road) and 'Lounge' to what the US *Billboard* charts now categorise as 'Adult Contemporary' – I like it all. I can't say I 'love' it all, not as I have loved orchestral and instrumental easy listening music from that very early age. But still, it is there as the 'soundtrack' to most adult lives in and out of the home.

(And, of course, it brings back to me treasured childhood memories of the best times spent with my late mother).

Overview

John Lennon is famously quoted as saying, 'before Elvis, there was nothing'. He could just as easily have said that before General Squier, there was nothing. Lennon is also said to have remarked he often listened to easy listening music when 'The Mrs' (Yoko Ono) was out.

Beginnings

Where did easy listening music come from? Inevitably, like so much pop music around the modern world, it has its roots in American popular culture, which really means that it grew out of the advent of the invention of radio and recorded music. Perhaps the man most responsible for its birth is strangely from the American military. His name is General George Squier and he, after an illustrious career inventing and improving military communications in the first decades of the 20th Century, came up with the idea of piped – or 'wired', as they called it then – music. His original idea was that musical notes and scales could be used as code to transmit secret messages between military command and the battlefront. He wasn't alone in his thinking and other inventors, notably in France, were thinking along the same lines. General Squier's thinking, however, went further. If music could be 'wired' for the benefit of the military, could it not be harnessed to bring music into the lives of people in the world at large? Radio was still very much in its infancy; radio sets were expensive and reception was still 'scratchy', but, thanks to inventions patented by General Squier, wired transmission allowed for quality transmission and reception.

Whether or not he'd read the books is unknown, but the idea of using music through radio technology to ease the tedium of commerce and industry in the modern world was not new in the storytelling of dystopian literature. Writers like Aldous Huxley had pictured a world where every aspect of people's lives was controlled by the State. One of the ways in which this was achieved was through the 'broadcasting' of music that influenced and even shaped how people thought and acted. Music was to be what, in modern parlance, might be called the 'soundtrack' of the totalitarian functioning of society. General Squier's thinking was, however, of a much kinder and simpler notion than this. 'Background music', as he thought of it, could make people's lives more pleasant than they had become in the industrialised world of the new age: music could be 'piped' down telephone lines into people's homes, the places where they worked, and into retail shops, hotels, restaurants, airports and so on. Music could be composed to suit particular backgrounds and ambient atmospheres. It was originally called 'Wired Radio'. However, General Squier thought this far too prosaic a term. Playing around with words, he took the words 'music', obvious, and 'Kodak', less so – except that the Kodak corporation had given the masses cheap and easy photography – and came up with the word 'Muzak'.

General Squier sold his patents to a company called the North American Company, which in turn created Wireless Radio Inc. The company piped music into their customers' homes, charging them for it through their electricity bills. After Squier's coining of the word Muzak, the company changed its name and the brand 'Muzak' was born.

Technological advances quickly made radio available at affordable prices and by the mid-1930s, households began receiving free broadcasts that were funded, not by consumer subscriptions, but by advertising. Over the next decades, the brand 'Muzak' evolved into what we know it as today: essentially, commercially manufactured music that is heard in public and workplaces.

A music business needs composers, arrangers, musicians, band leaders and orchestras. There were plenty of such people hungry for any kind of work. It wasn't long either before record companies cottoned on to the idea that there was an opportunity here for selling albums of what was beginning to be called 'mood music'. Radio was one thing, but it didn't enable people to play music in the home suited to particular domestic occasions. And the world itself was changing. The 1940s brought the horror of the Second World War. It ended, but the world had been through hell and back and now peace and harmony were wanted. Jazz and all its derivatives were great, but it was intrusive. It demanded your attention; it wanted you to dance or, at the least, tap your feet. In the home, something a little less demanding was needed. *Muzak* outside the home encouraged you to go with the flow of organised society, but in the home, modern consumerism was creating a world of colour and artistic design that could be personalised to suit one's own individual tastes. Domestic appliances were taking the drudgery out of housework, leaving people with much-increased leisure time. Mood music gave a soundtrack to accompany this stylishly new, leisured and increasingly affluent world.

The first mood music recording came out on Capitol Records in 1949. It was composer, arranger, bandleader and A&R director at Capital Records, Paul Weston's *Music For Dreaming*. He is reported as saying that 'as Frank Sinatra and Doris Day became more famous than the bands, the tunes got slower and slower. Jitterbugging went out, and my albums stepped into the gap…' It is telling that the first mood music album, which achieved great popularity and sold well, should be pointedly for 'dreaming'. Background music was becoming foreground music. Weston had included in the album, which incidentally was released as eight songs on four 78-rpm shellac records in a box set, such popular songs as 'I Only Have Eyes For You', 'I'm in The Mood For Love' and 'My Blue Heaven'. Weston himself described the arrangements as 'underplayed'. But what made the arrangements so 'dreamy' was the addition of strings to what was basically traditional orchestration, as opposed to the jazzy constructions of big band orchestras of the Swing Era, where violins were noticeable more by their absence than their presence.

I have said *Music For Dreaming* was issued in the old 78-rpm format in a photo album design typical of the time. Advances in audio technology led to

Columbia introducing the long-playing record in 1948. In supplanting 78-rpm records, which only allowed for a few minutes of playback – hardly enough time to create an uninterrupted mood – the LP provided enough time to create the kind of lingering atmosphere Paul Western wanted.

Weston released a number of follow-up LP albums with such titles as *Music For Memories*, *Music For Romancing*, *Music For The Fireside* and *Music For Reflection*. Coronet magazine in 1950 labelled him 'Master of Mood Music'. That was it: 'mood music' defined in terms of popular music. A whole new genre of popular music had arrived. Weston said his music walked the fine line between respectable jazz and 'wallpaper' music. It seemed that this was precisely what the record-buying consumer wanted. However, it became even more obvious, as record sales of mood music went stratospheric, that what they, in fact, had turned on to was much closer to the feel of cool, chic contemporary interior design than the roaring cool of the hot, danceable jazz so popular in the preceding decades.

A man came onto the scene now who was one of the genre's most unlikely characters: Jackie Gleason. After a less than exciting career as a comedian in films and on TV, Gleason had started to think that perhaps his showbiz future lay in production rather than performance. He was advised by none other than Bing Crosby to take his showbiz ideas and set up a company of his own to exploit them. Despite lacking musical training and his inability to read music, he loved pop music and was cottoning on to contemporary musical trends. He claimed to have conceived the idea of an album of 'slow dream music' in 1941 (four years before Weston), 'but couldn't get anyone interested in it at the time'. It was this idea he had put to Bing Crosby.

In 1942, Gleason was cast in the film *Orchestra's Wives* starring Glen Miller. He got friendly with Miller's trumpet player Bobby Hacket and expressed the hope that they might collaborate on some ideas he had for a musical venture. By January 1952, Gleason was hosting a television show *Cavalcade Of Stars*. He was offered a three-year exclusive contract by CBS. Given something of a free hand, he saw an opportunity to follow up on his musical ambitions and he put together a 27-piece orchestra, calling the outfit 'Music For Lovers Only'. His orchestra combined an oversized string section and Bobby Hacket's underplayed trumpet-playing moody arrangements of love-song standards. It is likely that Gleason was not unaware of the huge success Paul Weston was enjoying with his mood music albums. Lacking, as has been said, musical training, Gleason was nevertheless able to pick out musical themes on the piano, which he was able to communicate to his producers, Peter King and then George Williams, both of whom built an easy musical rapport with him. Gleason got what he was groping for: music to put his listeners in the mood for love. He said, '...when I heard music, I could listen to the sounds in the back of the melody and hear it all...' However, there still remained one problem: he could not get a recording label interested enough to record an album. In true visionary style, he funded the album himself.

When Bobby Hackett was asked what Gleason brought to the music, he replied: 'the checks'.

Gleason initially approached record company American Decca, but seeing him as a loud, clowning comedian, they didn't take him seriously as a music maker. Gleason's manager then persuaded Capitol Records – Paul Weston's label, which it will be remembered was doing very nicely out of his mood music albums – to take him on. In exchange for promoting his new show on CBS, *The Jackie Gleason Show*, Capitol agreed to let Gleason make an album, but on the condition that they didn't have to cover the costs. For anyone else, it might have been a no-no, but for Gleason, ever the entrepreneur, it was a gamble worth taking. He knew exactly what he wanted to create, even down to the design of the album cover, which he took great pains over, as he did with the entire creation of the album.

He called the album *Music For Lovers*. Upon release in 1953, it sold 500,000 copies and remained on the *Billboard* Top 10 charts for 153 weeks. Gleason went on to become a mood music tycoon, releasing in all over 40 albums.

First British Invasion

The Brits were always 'invading' US pop culture and giving it new directions: there was Henry Russell in the 19th century, and Stan Laurel, Charlie Chaplin, Bob Hope and P.G. Wodehouse, to name but a few of the early 20th century greats. In the field of mood music, hot on the heels of Paul Weston and Jackie Gleason, came Frank Chacksfield and Paolo Mantavani. In 1953, Chacksfield, born in 1914 in Battle, Sussex, went to number 2 in the US charts with his moody arrangement of 'Ebb Tide'. 'Ebb Tide' was a popular song written in 1953 by the lyricist Carl Sigman and composer Robert Maxwell. The song's arrangement emulates sea waves rising and falling on an ebb tide. But in Chacksfield's arrangement, it is not just movement, it is sensual movement, sexual in character even, especially if it is being played in the background of a romantic occasion. On the website www.spaceagepop.com, Chacksfield is quoted as saying:

> Orchestras are more than just a combination of sounds; they are not unlike people. Orchestras have moods and feelings, and above all, they can express those feelings. The best orchestras can make you angry and sad and even fall in love.

And again, it was all moodily enhanced with the introduction of a large string section into the orchestra. Chacksfield's predilection for layering, i.e. in recording parlance, overdubbing, was first given expression when he signed to Decca in 1953 and recorded his first big hit and golden record 'Terry's Theme', better known as 'Limelight', the title song from Charlie Chaplin's film of the same name. The success of 'Ebb Tide' earned him the *New Musical Express* 'Record of the Year' award. Mood music had arrived in the UK.

Someone who became an even bigger star than Chacksfield was Mantovani – Annunzio Paolo Mantovani, to be precise – except that, like Elvis, he became better known simply as 'Mantovani'. That tells you just how famous he did become. While not British by blood, he was brought up in England. Born in Venice in 1905, he moved with his parents to London in 1909. He was born into a musical family. His father, under the direction of the great Toscanini, had been the first violinist at the Scala Opera House in Milan. After moving to London, he was, for many years, concertmaster at London's Royal Opera House. Although steeped in classical music and being seen as something of a prodigy, Mantovani decided not to follow his father into a concert career, but instead to go into the world of popular band and orchestral music. Possessing charm and star quality, he quickly achieved a name for himself, first at the Metropole Hotel and later in cabaret at the Monseigneur's. But like so many of the great band leaders, he was groping to find a sound that was entirely his own. He knew it had to involve strings and lots of them, but was still not quite there. He turned to Ronald Binge, who had played the accordion in his early band, The Tipica Orchestra. Binge, also a composer and arranger, had composed 'Sailing By' – still used today on BBC Radio 4 to introduce its legendary shipping forecast – a dreamy, atmospheric piece of music that has all the hallmarks of early mood music. Mantovani had been asked by Decca Records in the USA to make an album of waltzes. He asked Binge to help with the arrangements. Binge somehow knew what Mantovani was groping for and he came up with the arrangement for 'Charmaine', an unprecedented million-seller record that gave birth to what was to become known as the 'Mantovani sound': 'cascading strings' that flowed lushly in mesmerising fashion throughout and in and around the melody.

As was said earlier, the 'sound', however, could not have been created without the benefit of contemporary recording techniques. Mantovani's recording engineer from the early days was Arthur Lilley. He used multiple microphones to create what nowadays would be called a 'wall of sound' (think of Phil Spector) that enabled Mantovani's cascading strings to flow and echo tsunami-like in and around what were, in fact, mostly the simple melodies of familiar-sounding pop tunes. 'Charmaine' was, for instance, originally the theme music to a silent film, *What Price Glory*, composed by Erno Rapee. Guy Lombardo recorded it in 1927. It was a big hit at the time but had been largely forgotten until Ronald Binge resurrected it and rearranged it for Mantovani. In fact, most of the tracks recorded in and beyond the Golden Era of easy listening music were new arrangements of the hit pop songs of their various eras.

'Mood' Music Goes Viral

Paul Weston, Jackie Gleason, Frank Chacksfield, Mantovani and what was becoming a whole host of band-wagon jumpers and imitators had taken General Squier's inspired vision to a mainstream level that even he might not have dreamed of. And dreaming and fantasising were what the pop world and its audiences in the peace and prosperity of the post-war age seemed to be intent on doing. Seeing the money that was there to be made, record companies, in general, were beginning to take full advantage of a market hungry for stylish and chic products. In our contemporary age of dressed-down living, the television series *Mad Men* reminded us of just how stylish mid-20th-century living had become. An affluent consumer society had become as rich with as much disposable income as the privileged classes of bygone eras had been. Suddenly, we could all aspire to the nice things in life.

Record companies began to design their LP covers to reflect this new chic. In fact, Jackie Gleason, the consummate marketing man, as already said, designed his own early covers. Of his 1958 album *That Moment*, he said: 'I chose the colours for their psychological value. Pastels are simpatico with music. The pink of the girl's face is the flush of love, and the blue of the boy's face is the flush of emotion'. It is quite clear the man knew what he was doing: creating a world of romance and chic that his record-buying public could and did inhabit. Gleason even had Salvador Dali contribute designs for his album covers, in particular, the cover for_*Lonesome Echo*. Dali's cover art is as subdued and mellow as the music and contains symbols from his iconography, such as a butterfly.

As the record companies got themselves into gear to capitalise on the growing public appetite for mood music, they began issuing genre series. Consumers were creating beautiful homes, so they created a series around socialising in the home. Cameo Records put out an album called *An Exciting Evening At Home With The International Pop Orchestra*, whoever they may be. Probably jobbing musicians paid a one-off fee to perform for the recording. The cover shows a gathering of elegantly dressed and coiffured ladies engaged in smiling conversation, while a handsome young man, stylishly dressed, plays with what is obviously the very latest in high-fidelity record-playing equipment.

In 1957, RCA Camden put out an album, *Let's Have A Dance Party,* by Buddy Morrow and His Orchestra. Until now, Buddy Morrow did not have an orchestra. He was a highly thought-of trombone player who had worked with both Tommy Dorsey and Glenn Miller. But RCA needed orchestras to record their mood music and they asked him to create an orchestra to make mood music precisely for the purpose of making albums. The cover of *Let's Have A Dance Party* features a smiling, finger-clicking teenager high-kicking to music coming from a record consul with records and their sleeves scattered on the carpet in front of it, the inference being that 'this chick' is having a great time at home playing the records that are created to enable her to do just that. RCA also put out *Music To Work Or Study By*, *Music For Reading*, *Music For Dining* and *Music To Help You Sleep*, while Mercury put out *Music For A Rainy Night*, all, again, with stylish, mood-reflecting cover designs.

'Mood Music' Morphs Into 'Easy Listening'

Recording techniques evolved rapidly, with 'high fidelity' audio recording being introduced. High fidelity aimed to reproduce sound in the highest quality possible, revolutionising music enjoyment. Listeners could now immerse themselves in the nuanced authenticity of recordings, turning it into a popular domestic pastime. The era brought forth a renewed appreciation for the art of music, elevating it from mere entertainment. Record companies seized this opportunity, releasing albums that showcased the capabilities of high fidelity. This era marked a pinnacle in recorded music, enhancing the deep connection between listeners and their favourite tunes. Mercury put out a series called *Music To Live By*; UK Decca, a series of 'Phase 4 Stereo' releases. The cover of *Music To Live By* shows a happy, united family lounging in a stylish sitting room listening to what the album promised was music '...to fit your every mood, popular, jazz and classical, through the magic of Mercury Living Presence Sound'. MGM Records put out an album called *The Perfect Background Music For Your Home Movies* by The Metro Strings, and even Kodak (you will remember that General Squier, the inventor of Muzak, took the last two letters of 'Kodak' to make his composite word 'Muzak') put out an album, the first of a series, *Sounds 8 Background Music For Your Personal Movies – 12 Orchestral Moods, 13 Special Sound Effects*.

No longer was audio equipment used to just play records; it had become an integral part of the consumer's way of life. The kit itself was stylishly designed, either in individual parts – turntable, amplifier, speakers – or else was put into a stereogram cabinet that became a sophisticated piece of furniture in its own right.

And the music itself? It was becoming something you listened to for its own sake, rather than something you put on as pleasant background ('wallpaper') music suitable for whatever given occasion. In contrast to rock 'n' roll, for instance, that other new phenomenon in popular music – a hybrid of black rhythm and blues and the white country music of America's deep south – mood music was something the grown-up listening public, in contrast to rock 'n' roll's young audience, found easy to listen to. The man who is credited with bringing mood music from an aficionado audience to a mass popular audience is Percy Faith. While Elvis exploded onto the world stage, Percy Faith and His Orchestra kind of waltzed onto it. The apotheosis of Faith's smooth orchestrations was his 1959 arrangement of the Max Steiner and Mack Discant classic 'Theme from A Summer Place'. Yet, what was, in fact, so different about 'Theme From A Summer Place'? What marked it out as 'easy listening' rather than 'mood' music? It was simply that mood music, or Muzak, was now morphing into something that was to be 'listened' to, rather than being something simply to be 'affected' by. It still had to be 'unintrusive', but now it began to be something that caught your ear.

A New OK Choral

Although in this study we focus on orchestral easy listening as opposed to the great vocalists of the genre, one man did introduce the sound of singing voices into his orchestral arrangements of pop standards. Not as the lead vocal backed by an orchestra, but as 'a natural echo', a 'chorus invisible', a 'ghost' of a sound that embellished and enhanced the delight of popular music. That man was Ray Conniff. While Mantovani had talked of wanting to create 'an effect of overlapping sound' as though his orchestra was 'playing in a cathedral', he had not taken the voices of cathedral choirs and introduced them into popular music. Ray Conniff effectively did just that. It was while working with Columbia Records' head of A&R that Conniff honed a sound he'd been struggling to give birth to. Conniff later said:

> I was recording an album with Mitch Miller – we had a big band and a small choir. I decided to have the choir sing along with the big band using wordless lyrics. The women were doubled with the trumpets and the men were doubled with the trombones. In the booth, Mitch was totally surprised and excited at how well it worked.

Miller allowed Conniff to start making his own recordings with the arrangements of voice and orchestra he'd created. He had limited success with single 45s and it wasn't until Columbia realised that his sound lent itself more to albums than singles that he became really successful. His first album was *'S Wonderful,* issued by Columbia in 1957. Again, as was typical by now in the easy listening genre, it was a collection of pop standards that Conniff recorded with his orchestra, accompanied by his 'wordless' vocal chorus of four men and four women. Gone were the cascading and lush strings; in their place were the more brash sounds of the horns and woodwind sections of the orchestra doubled with the vivacious, but still measured rather than jazzy, choral voices singing what were simply, yet sophisticatedly, 'dah-de-dahs' and 'do-de-doos' to the music. It might have been something that people did themselves when listening to records, but to actually put it on a record was something very new, and somehow, again, people loved it.

Tickling The Ivories

Surprisingly, country music found a way into the world of what radio stations were soon to dub 'beautiful music'. Chet Atkins at RCA had invented a new, smoother sound in country music. It came to be called the 'Nashville Sound'. Rock 'n' roll had severely dented the record sales of honky-tonk music, the dominant style of country music throughout the 1950s. The 'Nashville Sound' was created to appeal to the older and now more urbanised country music fan. Like easy listening orchestral music, it used smooth strings and choruses, dispensing with the traditional fiddles and steel guitars. Floyd Cramer was Chet Atkins' primary pianist. Imitating the note-bending sound of a steel guitar, Cramer developed the 'slip-note' style of piano playing in which a passing note slides almost instantly into or away from a chordal note, creating a sound that still, however, retained what he called 'a kind of lonesome cowboy sound'. With added strings and Conniff's 'wordless' chorus, his self-composed record 'Last Date', released in 1960, became a huge hit around the world. His follow-up single 'On the Rebound' reached number one in the UK charts. Taking each year's top country and pop hits, Cramer went on to record dozens of albums which were loved by easy listening country and pop music fans alike around the world.

While the US had Floyd Cramer, England had Russ Conway. Pianists were always very popular, particularly in pubs, where a piano provided a kind of music-hall melodious background, picking out the melody of a tune and embellishing it with playful harmonics and overtones that had people toe-tapping. Russ Conway took the rough edges of this toe-tapping, barrelling style and made it his own, just as Cramer and Atkins had done with country music. He scored a number of big hits in the UK, most notably 'Side Saddle', 'China Tea' and 'Roulette'. But he could also play identifiably easy listening tunes, complete with lush strings and 'wordless' singers, particularly when accompanied by Tony Osborne, Phillip Green, Michael Collins and their respective Orchestras, along with groups like The Williams Singers. He covered songs like 'Theme From a Summer Place', 'Passing Breeze', 'Always', 'The Warsaw Concerto', 'Ebbtide' and many other up-and-coming easy listening classics. He also made albums of pop hits, notably *The New Side Of Russ Conway*, released in 1971, that included songs like 'Up, Up and Away', 'Little Green Apples', 'My Way', 'Something', 'Somewhere My Love' and so on. While his toe-tapping hits remained ever-popular, his easy listening albums contained no hint of his bar-barrelling style and were equally popular, along with his personal sell-out appearances at venues like The London Palladium, on TV and radio.

Also, hugely popular on the ivories in England was Mrs Mills. She played singalong songs in a stride piano style. Strictly speaking, she might not be described as easy listening, except perhaps in the context of happy, catchy tunes that people loved to hear and which brightened up their lives.

Trinidadian Winfred Atwell was yet another hugely popular pianist in Britain and Australia. Again, her easy listening credentials might be questioned as her playing style was mainly boogie-woogie and ragtime, but she did release equally well-received and what only can be described as easy listening albums, complete with 'wordless' choir, with songs like 'As Long As He Needs Me', 'C'est L'amour', 'Greensleeves', 'Bewitched, Bothered and Bewildered', 'Soft Summer Breeze', 'Smile' and so on. She did have one US hit with 'Moonlight Gambler', which went to number 16 on the *Billboard* pop chart. While being slightly jaunty, it can nevertheless only be described as easy listening, with its choir sounding as hauntingly otherworldly, as the song's title might suggest it should.

Talking of the US, we have to mention Liberace. Known particularly for his high-camp flamboyancy, he played in an irresistibly straight, easy listening piano style. His albums included pop hits, show tunes and popularised classical music pieces by such composers as Liszt and Chopin, which were derisively dismissed as 'pure fluff' by serious critics of classical music, even though his audiences lapped them up. His 45-rpm single releases sold over 300,000 copies each, and his albums sold millions, gaining him six gold records. His syndicated television shows were equally popular. Looking straight into the camera, he would crack jokes and chatter away, making each of his often normally 30,000,000-strong viewers feel as if he was talking just to them. His stage settings and costumes were as over-the-top as they could be, but behind it all was his unmistakably easy listening piano style.

Playing not one but two pianos were the duo, Ferrante and Teicher. They had top ten hits with 'Theme From The Apartment', 'Theme From Exodus', 'Tonight' and 'Midnight Cowboy'. Minus Liberace's camp theatricals, they could be as equally flamboyant in their performances, which, playing with and off one another in a sparklingly inventive way, they preferred to call 'two-man show(s)'. They were classically trained and had experimented with the avant-garde, releasing albums *Blast Off!* and *Heavenly Sounds in Hi-fi*. They were interesting 'art' experiments, but they did not make money. Then they met renowned Muzak arranger Nick Perito at United Artists, who suggested that, if they wanted to make a living out of their music, they should add orchestral and choral backing to their playing. It was a short leap from there to easy listening arrangements, which, as they said, meant '…we no longer have to teach to make a living'. Their 1970 hit single rendition of Bob Dylan's 'Lay Lady Lay', clearly demonstrates, however, that by adding a reverberated guitar and brass, they still liked to mix it up with inventive instrumentation. Such playfulness with their music made their 'two-man shows' hugely popular and they sold millions of albums. It must be apparent by now that the latter was true with easy listening music in general. Many of its artists out-sold even the top rock and pop artists of the day, and many of their recordings still continue to sell steadily.

Again, playing not one but two pianos, was England's Ronnie Aldrich. Yes, *two* pianos, or so it appeared on his records. In fact, he was only playing one. In 1961, UK Decca Records invented what was called 'Phase 4 Stereo' (more on this later), which enabled Aldrich to produce some wonderful easy listening albums for Decca's Phase 4 Stereo Series, starting with *Melody And Percussion For Two Pianos* in 1961 and culminating in his 1978 release *Emotions*. There were no pyrotechnics, as was often found in the playing of Ferrante and Teicher, but just the ability to make his two hands sound like four. Behind him was a sophisticated backdrop of lush strings and orchestral instruments he knew easy listening audiences delighted in.

From There To Everywhere

While 'Muzak' continued along its bland and rather one-dimensional way, easy listening music, like an exploding firework, continued to light up the music worldwide in a variety of pleasing ways. Alongside the founding giants of the genre, there were, as always, the lesser gods. Record companies hurried to record these bands, thus making available a whole variety of easy listening music to suit the musical tastes of what was the beginning of a global world culture. It hailed firstly, as we know, from America, which was, anyway, a melting pot of all the world's tribes, particularly regarding the countries of eastern, western, northern and southern Europe, as well as Africa and Latin America. However, while it is true that America gave the world pop music, once arrived on foreign shores, it was often reinvented and sent straight back, as with The Beatles, The Rolling Stones, The Kinks, Santana and countless other groups and artists in the world of pop and rock music. As we have said, in the world of easy listening, England had given America Mantovani and Frank Chacksfield and Canada had given it Percy Faith. Now it was the turn of Germany, and Bert Kaempfert with 'Wonderland By Night' was the man.

The golden era's biggest star, certainly in terms of record sales and live audience attendance, was also from Germany. His name was James Last. His name was known to music lovers across the worlds of pop and classical music. He either made you want to put your fingers down your throat, or he filled you with varying degrees of pure delight. He might have even made you want to give expression to that sense of euphoria by getting up and taking your loved one in your arms and, well, looking her or him in the eye, seeing there a reflection that told you, yes, they loved you and all was sublimely right with the world. Last's record sales topped well over 200 million worldwide, winning him 200 gold and fourteen platinum discs. This was despite his music being dismissed by critics as 'acoustic porridge' and he himself as 'the king of elevator music'.

James Last's trademark, not surprisingly, was 'happy music'. His most popular albums were orchestrated collections of non-stop hit records, given a gently driving bass beat (he was an award-winning bass player in Germany long before he groped his way into easy listening success at Polydor Records), irresistibly backed by Ray Conniff's invention, the 'wordless' choir. Last's choir, however, were not 'instrumentalised' in the way Ray Conniff's were, but rather they gave a listener the sense that it was the sound of people at a gathering partying and singing along to the latest hits, quote again the Anglo-Saxon poem 'Solomon and Saturn': '...relieve(d) the heart's mood of every man ...heal(ed) the distress of daily living...'. And this was the job of all easy listening music, not least of all in terms of how it was marketed by its record companies, and they, of course, knew their marketing demographic well. Last achieved his first British success in 1967 with the album *This Is James Last,* which remained in the charts for 48 weeks, peaking at number six.

As well as selling millions of records, James Last and his Orchestra toured the world, giving sell-out concerts right up until practically the day he died. He and his orchestra appeared at the Albert Hall, London, no less than a staggering 90 times.

France, too, contributed to what was by now a worldwide popular music phenomenon. However, while the Germans had a tradition of 'oom-pa-pa' bands, which is probably what led to the music of a man like James Last, France was famed for love and romance. In 1967, Paul Mauriat had a number-one chart smash with 'Love is Blue'. 'L'amour est bleu' describes the pleasure and pain of love in colours. With its lush strings, Mauriat's arrangement owed more to Percy Faith than Ray Conniff. Sans vocals, it featured a harpsichord as its lead instrument. It was America's first instrumental number-one hit since 1963 (charting for seven weeks) and was France's only top seller in that country. It was originally the 1967 Eurovision Song Contest entry for Luxembourg by Greek singer Vicky Leandros (appearing as Vicky). While Leandros' version is a pleasant enough song to listen to, it didn't win the contest. The words are in French and so meant nothing to the English-speaking world. It plods along quite nicely without evoking any of the sentiments the lyrics suggest. However, in Paul Mauriat's hands, the tune, without its lyrics but with lush strings and harpsichord, soars into the realms of high romance in an irresistibly catchy arrangement that seductively draws the listener in.

Also from France came Jane Birkin's and Serge Gainsbourg's utterly sensational 'Je T'aime'. Its easy listening credentials might be called into question. But when covered by Ray Conniff, whose arrangement played down the original's sexual boldness, it became a firm favourite of easy listening lovers.

Birkin's and Gainsbourg's version, with its driving rock bass line and romantic strings, went beyond the bounds of mood and easy listening music. While mood and easy listening music never breached the boundaries of aural sensuality, 'Je T'aime' was inescapably sexy. Its lyrics contain the line 'Je vais et je viens, entre tes reins' ('I go and I come, between your loins'). Despite the sexual revolution of the swinging sixties, or perhaps because of it, it was a step too far for the Establishment: the record was banned in a number of countries. In the UK, the BBC would not allow it on its playlists, thereby necessarily making it a number-one hit single. It stayed on the charts for 31 weeks, something which must have given Britain's guardian of public morals, Mary Whitehouse, apoplexy. Gainsbourg originally recorded 'Je T'aime' with Brigit Bardot, but her embarrassed husband blocked its sales, considering it 'too hot' for even her steamy reputation. It didn't chart highly in America, though in 1969, the Hollywood 101 Strings Orchestra released a 7" single of it sans lyrics, on the A-side at least, calling it 'Love at First Sight'. On the B-side was a highly sexed version, still without words but with a woman, Bebe Bardon, the credits state, unmistakably sounding as if she is reaching what has to be called an 'orgasm'. How well the 45-rpm sold the present author has not been able to find out. On a last word, 'Je T'aime' is thought to have been the inspiration behind Donna Summer's equally sexy smash 1980s disco hit 'Love to Love You Baby'.

Also from France was Francis Lai, who composed, less sensationally, what has become another easy listening staple, 'A Man And A Woman', originally the theme music to the 1966 film of the same name. It has been said that 'no song captures the heart and soul of easy listening music' quite like this piece of romantic movie sweetness. To use the words 'schmaltz' would be to dimmish it, since it perfectly captures the mood of a love story that is so redolent of the lives of ordinary people.

Like so many of the composers, orchestra leaders and soloists of our genre, Lai had been around the music scene for some time before discovering where his true calling lay. It is probably while being an accompanist for the great chanteuse Edith Piaf, for whom he wrote songs, that he discovered the appeal of heart-tugging tunes. By adding Ray Conniff's 'wordless' choir and an upbeat Brazilian tempo to 'A Man And A Woman', he gave it the kind of appeal that is timeless. To this day, the piece continues to be used to enhance the romantic atmosphere of countless films, television shows and dramas around the world.

Lai also wrote the theme music to what this time was a devastatingly tragic, if romantic, film, *Love Story*, which tells the tale of a young love that has had to sacrifice so much but which is cut short by terminal cancer. The film is considered by the American Film Institute to be one of the top ten most romantic films ever made and is one of the highest-grossing films of all time. Lai's theme music for the film plays no small part in this, making it not just one of the great movie themes of all time – it won him an Oscar and a Golden Globe Award, as well as giving him a number two-hit record in *Billboard*'s album chart – but also a staple of easy listening music, with its arrangement of lush strings and lilting solo piano.

Returning to England, there is one solo instrumentalist who must be mentioned and that is Acker Bilk. While ostensibly a jazz musician, he produced what is perhaps the moodiest of all smooth, easy listening tunes, 'A Stranger On the Shore'. In 1962, it was a huge hit on both sides of the Atlantic, remaining on the English charts for 55 weeks, peaking at number two, while staying at number one on the US *Billboard* charts for seven weeks and then remaining on the chart for another 21 weeks. Never changing his style, Bilk went on to make top-selling EPs and albums such as *A Taste Of Honey* (1963) and *Mood For Love* (1966), covering easy listening classics and the hits of the day. Backed by a string ensemble, his arrangements complimented anything done by Mantovani and Percy Faith.

Italy also gave easy listening music a timeless gem. 'More' was the 1962 theme music to an Italian cult documentary, *Mondo Cane*, which in English means 'dog world'. It was a documentary which gave glimpses of what life was like culturally in different parts of the world. An international hit, it was initially intended to shock Italy's catholic viewing public, with its scenes of fast life and liberality. Surprisingly, given the content of the film, 'More' was as romantic a tune as you will find, and when words (by Ciorciolini Marcello and Oliviero Gaetano) were put to it, it became a passionate love song, as the first verse amply illustrates:

More than the greatest love the world has known,
This is the love I'll give to you alone.
More than the simplest words I try to say,
I only live to love you more each day.

The music was composed by Nini Rosso and Riz Ortolini. 'More' won a Grammy Award and earned an Oscar nomination for Best Original Song, but it was Kai Winding, a Danish-born trombonist, and his Orchestra who took it to the top of the *Billboard* chart in the US, where it remained at number two for four weeks, and on the chart for thirteen.

Italy also gave the world Ennio Morricone. He wrote Hugo Montenegro's worldwide hit 'The Good, the Bad and the Ugly', which is, of course, his more rhythmic arrangement of the theme tune to Sergio Leone's classic spaghetti western of the same name, starring American actor Clint Eastwood as the 'man with no name'. Ennio Morricone's music, with its mellifluous trumpet solos, 'wordless' vocals interspersed with evocative macho and cowboy-like utterances, is hauntingly exotic in a way lovers of easy listening music can't resist, even though the music is full of pathos rather more than romance.

Ennio Morricone wrote hundreds of film scores, many of which remain as popular around the world as 'The Good, the Bad and the Ugly'. Morricone purists might argue that easy listening arrangements of his music tame it rather, but it cannot be doubted that the music, even when played by Morricone himself, carries the listener along effortlessly.

The 'Latin' Thing

The musical rhythms and dance beats of Latin America influenced American popular music long before the arrival of easy listening music, particularly in dance music. What it is that constitutes 'Latin American music' is hotly debated by its aficionados. Largely, it is a term used by the music industry as a catch-all term to describe the various styles of music created in the US that are inspired by older South American Spanish and Portuguese musical genres. 'Tex-Mex', 'Tejano' and 'Merengue' are perfect examples. They gave to the US and then the world the 'Latin' dance crazes for the bosa nova, the tango, the pasa doble, rumba, cha-cha, samba, salsa, bachata and so on. At the heart of Latin music is rhythm, in all its sensuality and even sexiness. But, as in all popular music, there is also melody and harmony, which is where, outside of the dance itself, lies the easy-music aspect of it. Herb

Albert is often described as the godfather of Latin easy listening. He was an immensely successful American vocalist and trumpet player who led his band, The Tijuana Brass, in the 1960s. His inspiration for his sound came following a visit to a bullfight in Tijuana, Mexico, where he watched the spectators being thoroughly roused by a mariachi band of brass musicians. He set out to recreate the sound in a pop record. Having set up a recording studio in his garage at home, he took a song written by Sole Lake called 'Twinkle Star', overdubbed its intro with the sound of cheering bullfight spectators and added 'wordless' female singers, while playing a slightly out of sync smooth trumpet solo. Changing the song's name to 'The Lonely Bull', it gave him a Top Ten hit in 1962. An album of the same name quickly followed, which peaked at number six on the *Billboard* album charts. He had financed and distributed the record himself, forming A&M Records in the process. Albert went on to have numerous hit singles and albums, featuring more compositions by Sole Lake and covering hit songs of the day with his Mexican-mariachi sound.

Next followed the 1962 Brazilian top five hit record 'The Girl From Ipanema', or in its original Portuguese, 'Garota de Ipanema'. A sultry, jazzy bosa nova song, it was written in 1962 with music by Antônio Carlos Jobim and Portuguese lyrics by Vinícius de Moraes. It was a 1965 worldwide hit for Stan Getz, reaching number five on the US *Billboard* charts and winning a Grammy for Record Of The Year. Although Getz's version features a vocalist, 'The Girl From Ipanema' has been recorded by numerous easy listening orchestras, not least of all by Percy Faith and His Orchestra on his Latin-inspired 1965 album *Latin Themes For Young Lovers*. It is the second most recorded pop song in history, beaten only by The Beatles' song 'Yesterday'.

Easy listening Latin was, however, fully established worldwide the following year by another Brazilian, Sergio Mendes, with his hit album *Herb Alpert Presents Sergio Mendez And Brazil '66*. Mendes and his band successfully auditioned for Herb Alpert's A&M Records. Albert himself played no small part in the production of the music on the album. By adding his name to its title, he guaranteed it would grab people's attention.

My namesake, The Beatles press officer Derek Taylor, wrote in the sleeve notes to the album that Sergio Mendes had created: 'with considerable taste a delicate blend of piano jazz, subtle Latin undertones, with borrowings from Lennon and McCartney and Mancini.' Although Mendez uses a mixture of 'wordless' and lyric singing female voices singing in English and Portuguese, the vocals are more part of the instrumentation than anything that might be called a lead vocal. The music itself is stylishly seductive, with catchy arrangements of a bosa nova rhythm on top of Mendes's piano playing. There is a cover of The Beatles' 'Day Tripper' and two Henri Mancini songs. 'Mas Que Nada', the album's opening track, reached number four on the US *Billboard* charts and stayed on the chart for seventeen weeks. Sergio Mendes and Brazil '66 scored a number-one US *Billboard* hit in 1968 with a similarly Latin-cool cover of The Beatles' song 'Fool On the Hill'. Latin dance had become listenable, rather than just danceable, and very easily began to slot into an easy listening mode.

The Brits Invade Again

Just as Elvis had changed the mood of popular music, giving it attitude, along came The Beatles, who brought back melody and harmony. Rock 'n' roll had undoubtedly been the new musical form that grabbed the imagination of teenagers in the UK, as it had young people in the US. However, by the time it arrived on UK shores, it had matured into the more commercially acceptable music of Buddy Holly and The Crickets. While Elvis was sex on demand, Buddy Holly was rhythm, beat and romance all rolled into one. The Beatles absorbed this in a polite English way, creating a 'nicer', if still essentially beaty kind of music. When dressed up in suits by their manager Brian Epstein, The Beatles gave back to America a more palatable kind of pop music, whose mass appeal embraced again, not just the young, but also the grown-up world. There could not have been Beatle music without the rhythm 'n' blues and country music of the deep South of America that Elvis Presley had turned into the white man's brew called 'rock 'n' roll'. It was the sound Sam Phillips of Sun Records, who had discovered Elvis, famously said he had been looking and waiting for. There was not, however, only Beatles music; there was a whole slew of British bands changing the face of popular music, and not just in America, but across the world, and the easy listening brand of popular music was not immune to it.

Before he became king of the golden era in the later decades of easy listening, in 1965, James Last put out an album unabashedly called *Beat In Sweet*. The album creates a whole new world of easy listening covers of contemporary pop hits. While remaining faithful to the beat tempo of the original songs like Sony and Cher's 'I Got You Babe', The Righteous Brothers' 'You've Lost That Lovin' Feelin'', Barry McGuire's 'Eve of Destruction' and Bob Dylan's 'Mr Tambourine Man' and 'Like a Rolling Stone', he infused his arrangements with all the trademarks we have come to expect of orchestral/instrumental easy listening arrangements, particularly lush strings. Yet where authentication of a new pop sound is required, he further infused his arrangements with guitars, mouth organ and drums, making them sound as contemporary as the original hits themselves.

More conventionally but nevertheless in the new mode, in 1966, Percy Faith and His Orchestra released an album of contemporary pop hits called *Themes For The "In" Crowd*. Black rhythm 'n' blues singer Dobie Grey had a hit record in 1965 called 'The In Crowd', whose lyrics sang of someone who was as inclusively 'hip' as anyone could be. The first track on Percy Faith's album was indeed 'The In Crowd'. His trademark strings were still there, but added to it now, as with all the tracks on the album, was the 'beat' of the new music. It was still intended to be music for 'dreamers' and 'lovers' but for 'dreamers' and 'lovers' of a new generation.

Even Jackie Gleason, who released his groundbreaking album of what was then called 'mood' music in 1953, and still ever one to jump on a new commercial bandwagon, released an album in 1968 called *Now Music...For Today's Lovers*. His arrangements were as dreamy as ever, but along with his lush strings were, again, guitars, even a sitar, and drumbeats. There had to be if the 'now sound' of the title was to hold any relevance to a new generation. Gone from the front cover of the album's sleeve was a photograph of a romancing young couple. Instead, in its place, is an impressionistic drawing of Gleason holding said sitar. A changed world indeed.

New Kids On The Block

From The Beatles' album *Rubber Soul* onwards, pop music was no longer just about love and romance and began to be as much about the meaning of life. 'Love' was still there, but it was more about brotherly love, the sort that goes with 'peace and love'. The song on the album that reflects this is 'The Word'. A John Lennon song, it talks about discovering such love. It's worth quoting select lyrics because the song really does harbinger a new direction in pop music:

In the beginning, I misunderstood,
But now I've got it, the word is good,
Spread the word and you'll be free,
Spread the word and be like me,
Spread the word I'm thinking of,
Have you heard the word is love?

Gone in the song are boys and girls gripped by romance and the urge to procreate. In its place is mysticism. Then, there is the penultimate song eight tracks later: 'In My Life'. It is a song about time and place and nostalgia. A new generation, a post-war generation, had discovered that life was about an awful lot more than just getting married, settling down and having kids. Music was changing, and with it, easy listening music changed.

In 1961, *Billboard* in America created a new chart for easy listening music single record sales. Although by now, the best sellers were beginning in the main to feature easy listening vocalists, orchestral music was still there. Number three in the top-selling records for 1961 was Lawrence Welks' 'Calcutta' (London Records – 45-HLD 9261). In 1968, he again had a hit with 'Green Tambourine', a dreamy, psychedelic song about playing a green tambourine, first released by American singing group The Pied Pipers and then by Britain's Status Quo. In Welk's version, there was still the 'wordless' choir invented by Ray Conniff, but as the decade wore on, choruses began more and more to sing the lyrics. In 1967, Conniff himself put out an album in which his choir sang the words to Simon and Garfunkel's song 'The 59th Street Bridge Song (Feelin' Groovy)'. And gone, too, in this arrangement were the lush strings. In their place was simply an ensemble of easy-going instrumentation, with, again, the emphasis on the beat.

This set the tone for easy listening orchestral music from here on. In 1967, The Beatles released their seminal album *Sgt Pepper's Lonely Hearts Club Band*. The year before, on the other side of the Atlantic, The Beach Boys released *Pet Sounds*. Both albums were studio albums and both bands were feeding off and competing with one another in terms of creating music that went beyond ordinary pop. Drugs played a part in both bands' compositions, but there was also an ever-expanding world of recording technological wizardry. If the long-player 33 1/3 LP had been a gift to Paul Weston and Jackie Gleason, the Mellotron, the Moog synthesiser and multi-layer recording had given 1960s pop groups their wings. Marijuana and LSD did indeed play their part, but the technology was the thing that allowed pop to give expression to its ever-expanding mind. And where pop went, easy listening continued to follow. All through easy listening's golden era, orchestra leaders and arrangers had adapted pop hits. They knew it was integral to their success. This fact was not lost on the newcomers to the genre, and particularly not their record companies.

While the older band leaders and their orchestras still went their conventional way with hit songs like Ray Conniff's rendition of 'Somewhere My Love (Lara's Theme)', and Henri Mancini's 'Love Theme from Romeo and Juliette', both number one for weeks on end, other orchestras like The Hollyridge Strings and those of Paul Mauriat, Raymond Lefevre, Frank Pourcel and Caravelli (Claude Vasori) began now to enter into that cosmic, 'far-out' world of 1960s and 1970s pop.

There's a fine line to be drawn between what remains an easy listening arrangement of a pop song and what becomes an infinitely more involved, almost classical-music type of orchestration. Paul Mauriat often crossed that line with individual Beatles songs like 'Penny Lane'. His arrangement is too 'busy' for a pop song and, even in terms of a piece of light classical music, too energised to be anything like the mood music easy listening had evolved out of. It had strayed too far from the unobtrusiveness of background music, instead demanding in all its sophisticated musicality to be carefully listened to. Yet, when Mauriat re-arranges a song like 'Ticket to Ride' or 'Michelle', he can make it fit almost perfectly into an easy listening mode. It might be because it's a love song, whereas 'Penny Lane' strives to create a colourful image of city life, with all its hustle and bustle and sights and sounds.

American Mike Curb, with his group, the 'Mike Curb Congregation', couldn't have appeared to stray further from what constitutes easy listening music. However, with barely the use of an orchestra and certainly, without lush strings, he created a sound that could only be described as remaining smoothly unobtrusive. Using a Ray Conniff style chorus but with words (remember Conniff had formed his own lyric-singing chorus in 1969), he produced a brace of hit singles in 1970, followed by an album that fits easily into an easy listening mode. The hit singles were 'Ginger Bread Man' and 'Burning Bridges', the latter being the theme tune to the zany Clint Eastwood, Donald Sutherland and Terry Savalis WWII film *Kelly's Heroes*, in which a motley crew of GI's go AWOL behind enemy lines to rob a French bank of a fortune in gold bars. The song 'Burning Bridges' tells the story of a man who would have had a happier life if he had heeded the warnings of his friends and stayed home. The melody, sung by Curb's choir-like 'congregation', has a kind of gentle fatefulness about it that nevertheless creates that smoothly unobtrusive sound, carrying the listener along without really taking him or her out of themselves. Throughout the album, named for the song, and featuring pop songs such as Crosby, Stills, Nash and Young's 'Teach Your Children Well', The Beatles' 'Let it Be' and even the rock gospel song 'Spirit in the Sky' by Norman Greenbaum, Curb manages to sustain a no less easy listening feel, perhaps even achieving the cathedral-like choir sound that Mantovani had aspired to create way back in the mid-1950s.

Yet, when Italy's Caravelli and His Magnificent Strings arranged The Beach Boys' 'I Can Hear Music', it became beautifully easy listening simply because he did not leave out the lush strings. The same is true of the Hollyridge Strings' arrangement of 'Don't Worry Baby'. In the right hands, mind-expanding rock can, in its essence, be turned into something even grown-ups uninvolved with pop's more searching side can enjoy.

At around the time that The Beach Boys and The Beatles were creating *Pet Sounds* and *Sgt Pepper's Lonely Hearts Club Band,* respectively, an equally new direction was being taken in easy listening music by Leo Kulka, Brad Miller and Don Ralke. Leo Kulka was fascinated by natural sound and, in 1961, had one night recorded a violent storm that was raging outside his bedroom window. Thereafter, he played it when wanting to relax. In 1964, he opened a studio in San Francisco where he began to experiment with mixing his thunderstorm recording, wind-chimes, percussion and other sound effects with music. He timed the thunder bursts to coincide with musical crescendos. In 1965, Kulka teamed up with sound effects whiz Brad Miller to create, on a four-track stereo recorder, a series of equally weird and wonderful sounds. They persuaded the management of the San Francisco Airport's Hilton Hotel to let them play the sounds in the hotel's top-floor cocktail bar. They supplemented the sounds with a synchronised light show and effusions of various atmospheric perfumes and smells. Patrons became so mesmerised, even 'spaced-out' by the experience that they stopped drinking, which was not at all to the management's liking and Kulka's and Miller's show was enlivened with a rock band, which, as Kulka himself said, simply disrupted and spoiled the experience. They lost the gig.

Then, one evening, a DJ friend of the pair decided to play their tapes live on San Francisco's FM stereo radio station KFOG, where he had a program and a free hand in what he played. He is reputed to have synchronised the tapes with easy listening music – was it Paul Weston's album *Music For A*

Rainy Night? – playing both in full FM stereophonic sound. Listeners loved it and the studio phones lit up with listeners phoning in to say how evocative of romantic times past and new the 'music' was. Listeners were asked to name the group behind the sounds and they came up with the name 'Mystic Moods Orchestra'. Seeing how popular their musical creation was, Kulka and Miller decided to try and get a record deal. Mercury turned them down and they tried Phillips' Records. Kulka says that their A&R man came to see them in a thunderstorm. Failing to find a cab, the man and his wife arrived to see Kulka to talk about his tapes soaked to the bone. Indignant rather than impressed, the man seemed to think it was a bad omen. His wife thought otherwise and told him to just 'shut up and listen to the tapes'. The result was that Mystic Moods Orchestra got a record deal. Arranger Don Ralke was brought in to take care of what was the essential easy listening music side of the recordings, even including some of his own compositions, and the album *One Stormy Night*, recorded at Gold Star, the studio Phil Spector famously used, was the outcome. Included amongst the tracks are the sort of pop standards easy listening fans had come to expect. Songs such as 'Autumn Leaves', 'Sayonara' and, strangely, a folk tune, 'Minstrel Boy'. The music arrangements were pretty much as you'd expect, but with Kulka's and Miller's storm sound effects added, they became something quite moodily different, some even said disturbing rather than soothing. That is, until the music itself actually comes in. Different and perhaps not as 'far-out' as the music created by The Beach Boys on *Pet Sounds* and The Beatles on *Sgt. Pepper's Lonely Hearts Club Band*, *One Stormy Night*, released both in the UK and the US, became a minor pop success and, reaching a not-yet-hippy-but-soon-to-be audience, sold well. *Billboard,* in its 22 October 1966 edition, said of it in its Spot Poplight section:

> A beautiful album of ten melodic instrumentals played against a backdrop of a thunderstorm. This combination is a unique and emotional listening experience. Public response will be favourable and overwhelming, A natural for programming.

While not exactly 'overwhelming', the album did do well and reached number 63 in the chart. One wonders if The Beatles, in incorporating sound effects on the track 'Good Morning' on *Sgt. Pepper's*, which synchronises the clucking of a cockerel with the opening bars of the track, had heard the sounds of the Mystic Sounds Orchestra while touring in the U.S. Similarly, had Pink Floyd been so inspired when recording *Dark Side Of The Moon* and their other albums which incorporate sound effects? It is also to be remembered that Frank Chacksfield used sound effects on 'Ebbtide' and Herb Alpert used them on 'The Lonely Bull', admittedly neither quite as weirdly. In terms of easy listening music, Kulka, Miller and Ralke's innovations did not catch on.

The More Things Alter, The More They Stay The Same

From the 1960s and 1970s on, pop music branched off into so many musically rich and innovative directions that it must have been hard for easy listening orchestras and arrangers to keep up, but most did manage to do so. I have already mentioned Jackie Gleason's 1968 album *Now Music… For Today's Lovers*. Mantovani, too, recorded an album of the era's hits on his posthumous 1982 album release, *A Journey Into Digital Sounds*. The songs are given his trademark 'cascading strings' treatment but sound no less familiarly pop-orientated for that. He includes Beatles songs, as well as Roberta Flack's 'Killing Me Softly With His Song', Harry Neilson's 'Without You' and Bette Midler's 'The Rose'. All sound very contemporary.

Frank Chacksfield was also still out there conducting and covering a plethora of pop singles and hit album tracks, from Tamla Motown's The Commodores' 'Three Times A Lady' and The Temptations' 'My Girl', to soul music's Otis Reading's 'Dock Of The Bay'; from The Beatles' John Lennon song 'Come Together', to Simon and Garfunkel's 'Mrs Robinson' and 'Bridge Over Troubled Waters'; from Jim Webb's 'MacArthur's Park' to Crosby, Still and Nash's 'Marrakesh Express', Scot McKenzie's 'San Francisco' and Johnny Cash's 'I Walk The Line', as well as the songs of Donavon, Bob Dylan, The Moody Blues, The Doors and many more.

There are also albums, such as the unlikely 1971 release *Tamla Meets Tijuana* by London group The Tequila Brass. It is a delightfully breezy arrangement of such Tamla classics as 'My Girl', 'How Sweet It Is', 'Up Tight', 'Baby I Need Your Loving' and 'The Tracks of My Tears'. There are no lush strings orchestration, but simply Mexican-style brass instruments, yet the sound is as pleasantly unobtrusive as you'd expect. The 'breeziness' of the arrangements does connote something of a festive feeling, but this does not detract from the easy listening mood of the album. In fact, it was this 'festive' feeling that was the very essence of the era's orchestra leader of greatest longevity and unstoppable multi, multi-million record sales, sales that at the time outstripped many pop and rock stadium artists and chart toppers. That man was, of course, and as already discussed above, Germany's James Last.

Throughout the late 1960s and 1970s, his music evolved into something quite unique in the world of easy listening music. By keeping up with whatever direction pop music moved in, he continued to attract concert audiences and record buyers alike, making him only second to Elvis Presley in terms of chart success. And not just in England but all around the world. Easy-listening purists, however, argue he was not easy listening at all. Despite this, it cannot be denied that his own compositions 'Happy Heart' and 'Music From Across The Way' were easy listening hits for Andy Williams, and his 'Fool' was similarly a hit for Elvis, while 'Games That Lovers Play', a hit for Eddie Fisher, has become an easy listening classic.

However, it was Last's live concerts that kept his music evergreen. For decades, they attracted tens of thousands of people of mixed generations who came to escape the angst of rock music to simply enjoy a pleasant evening of easy-going, non-stop, joyous music that even made some of them want to get up and dance. Was it easy listening music? If being 'happy' makes everything in life seem 'easy', then it undoubtedly was.

The Inbetweeners

There were a number of orchestras that were somehow in between Muzak and easy listening music. None of them were dazzlingly original in the way that the big stars above were, but they did produce some music that was pleasant enough to listen to, though more as something that remained in the very background. The best, and I mean the 'best' of easy listening music, could hold its own against anything in the pop charts. The chart toppers of all the solo artists, band leaders and their orchestras mentioned above brought something new and different to pop music, whereas what I call 'the inbetweeners' simply recreated what the chart toppers had created, with record companies and music business entrepreneurs cashing-in on a good thing and churning out release after release of albums and sometimes singles of worthwhile junk. It was probably this kind of output that gave easy listening music, in general, its pejorative reputation, not least of all because it was difficult to differentiate between what of this output was definably easy listening and what was demonstrably Muzak.

A perfect example of an 'inbetweener' outfit was 101 Strings. Between 1957 and 1981, they produced 150 albums, none of them uniquely original, but all of them produced to cash in on the marketability of both Muzak and its offspring easy listening music. The man responsible for the mega output of 101 Strings was American music mogul David L. Miller. It was he who, in the early 1950s, released, on his Essex Record label, Bill Haley and His Comets' rock 'n' roll records, turning the band from a fairly average country and western/western swing band into one of the originators of commercial rock 'n' roll success. Miller shifted his gaze next to the other new phenomenon in the music business: the rise of mood music. As with Jackie Gleason, dollar signs could be seen rolling in his eyes. Strangely, Miller found his studio orchestra in Hamburg, Germany, rather than in the US. He signed Orchester des Nordwestdeutschen Rundfunks conducted by Wilhelm Stephen to copy exactly what Paul Weston, Jackie Gleason, Mantovani and company had made such a great success of; that is, to record moody (easy listening) albums of pop standards, using everything they threw into the mix, particularly multi-layered lush and cascading strings. The records were going to be pressed in Miller's own plants and released through his own distribution channels, which meant through the main grocery shops rather than records shops, the traditional outlets for selling records.

Not one but three albums were released in November 1957, with another twelve albums being released in 1958. This was saturation selling on a grand scale. Not wanting to miss out on publishing revenue, Miller also got his staff arrangers to produce compositions so alike to the existing pop standards as to be virtually indistinguishable from the originals unless you were listening very carefully, which mood music record buyers were not noted for – the music being essentially definable as 'wallpaper music'. He also issued albums with international themes, such as *Gypsy Campfires*, *The Soul Of Spain*, *Hawaiian Paradise*, *I Love Paris*, *East Of Suez* and *Songs Of The Seasons In Japan*. They have been called 'musical travelogues', being designed to feed the imagination of a world that could be easily discovered through the means of relatively cheap commercial flights and affordable package holidays. Presumably, to give variety and make record buyers think they were buying something different, Miller also released records using different orchestra names, such as Cinema Sound Stage Orchestra and the Zero Zero Seven Band. The source of Miller's orchestral outfits, Orchester des Nordwestdeutschen Rundfunks, consisted of 126 musicians. His producers and recording engineers took full advantage of modern recording techniques to make what was described on the album sleeve notes as a playback experience rich in 'all the human ear can sense and hear'. Miller took as much trouble packaging his albums as was taken by all record companies in producing mood and easy listening music albums.

Miller sold what can only be called his 'franchise' in 1964. The new owners sought to keep up with the times by covering in Miller's safe and predictable arrangements the hits of the beat and rock decades of the 1960s and 1970s. The totality of record sales achieved by 101 Strings in the 24 years they were in existence was in excess of 50 million. They scored five hit albums in the UK: number nine with *Gypsy Campfires* (1958), number seven with *The Soul Of Spain* (1958), number ten with *Grand Canyon Suite* (1958), a number one with *Down Drury Lane To Memory Lane* (1960), which stayed on the chart for 26 weeks, and a number 32 with *Morning Noon And Night* (1983). 101 Strings did not perform live or tour.

It's Okay To Judge An Album By Its Cover

The long-playing vinyl record came into existence at about the same time as easy listening music began to evolve out of General Squier's mood music invention, Muzak. You will remember that Paul Weston's 1945 groundbreaking album *Music For Dreaming* came out first in a 78-rpm shellac four record box set. This was because one side of a 78-rpm record could only take one track. These 78-rpm box sets were in the codex shape of a photograph album and not an actual cardboard box as we knew it for LP sets and know it still for CD box sets. The 78-rpm album codex design was a standard already set, with the front cover generally being blank save for the name of the artist. Any other information regarding record label, catalogue number, track name, artist and composer name being printed on the record itself. Cover art was, however, coming in but was still not designed necessarily as a marketing tool. Against a background of red and white split colour decorated with star sparkle, a blue banner simply announces the album title, while an uneven note containing Paul Weston and his orchestra's name, with the track titles underneath, is placed at an angle above the banner slightly left of centre. It reflects the coming modernity of its decade, but nothing more. It's not particularly eye-catching and would not entice you to buy the album unless you were specifically there to do so. With the coming of the vinyl LP and a new age of demographic marketing, this was to be the precise purpose of album cover art.

It was at Columbia Records that the ubiquitous square album cover was invented. Even though vinyl was not brittle in the way shellac was, the fine grooves of vinyl LPs damaged easily, and record companies looked for an effective way of protecting them. It was Alex Steiner who solved the problem. Seen as an icon of mid-20th century utilitarian design, his invention of the square and flat sleeve didn't just protect the disc inside; it also made it easy to store albums, both in record shop shelving and display, as well as in the home. Where Columbia led, a whole industry followed.

Capitol Records issued *Music For Dreaming*, by common consent, the first easy listening album. Capitol Records was founded in 1942 in Los Angeles by Johnny Mercer, the man who famously wrote the words to 'Moon River', film producer Buddy de Sylva and record shop owner Glenn Wallichs. It was a modern company with modern ideas. In their 50th Anniversary book, they stated that:

> Trends were spotted early by discriminating designers and applied to record covers to grab the attention of the consumer as far back as Capitol's history extends. Innovative concepts in photography, illustration and graphic design led potential buyers to judge music by its covers. When drab album art was the norm, Capitol introduced colour, graphics and… sex appeal!

They did the latter with later reissues of *Music For Dreaming*. And as mentioned above, Jackie Gleason exploited Capitol's vision to the full.

In fact, it became the norm for album covers of all easy listening releases across all record labels to produce romantically mood-setting covers to reflect not just the genre but the mood an individual album was trying to induce in persuading a would-be purchaser to buy it. If it was evenings-in, there'd be a cosy, generally chic sitting or dining room featured, with laughing friends gathered around. If it was a quiet evening, there'd be a pretty, sometimes sexy-looking lady lying on the carpet in front of her radiogram looking through her albums, which would, of course, be a sampling of the particular record label's releases. Be it the sitting room, dining room or kitchen, everything in the home looked new and modern. If it was an album to reflect international travel, as with so many of 101 Strings releases, and other orchestras, there'd be an exotic cover to fire the imagination to make the record buyer want to travel to romantic or exciting holiday destinations.

A whole new industry arose for graphic artists to employ their talents. The use of modernist design was aimed at the modern consumer. Along with Alex Steinweiss at Columbia Records was Jim Flora and photographer S. Neil Fujita. Decca had Reid Miles, while Capitol had, along with a determined Gleason who, you will remember, commissioned Dali to create the cover art for *Lonesome Echo*, painter Thomas B. Allen and costume designer Donald Lee Feld, better known as 'Donfeld'. Mercury had David Stone Martin, Andy Warhol, Ben Shahn and Bob Cato.

Colour played an integral part in mid-century design, and this is seen in easy listening album cover design. There is a strong use of vibrant, pastel and muted blues, reds, pinks, yellows and greens, along with clean lines and often abstract shapes. Later graphic illustration gave way to photographic design and depiction of orchestra leaders, as can be seen, for instance, in the covers of Ray Conniff, Percy Faith and particularly James Last, as the identities of artists became synonymous with their music.

It wasn't just the front cover that was important, the back cover of the album was equally so. Jackie Gleason, for instance, used the back cover, not just to show the track list but sometimes to instruct the adult buyer on how to listen to his music. There is a picture of Gleason shaking hands with Dali and a quote from Dali saying how he conceived his design:

> The first effect is that of anguish, of space, and of solitude. Secondly, the fragility of the wings of a butterfly, projecting long shadows of later afternoons, reverberates in the landscape like an echo. The feminine element, distant and isolated, forms a perfect triangle with the music instruments and its other echo, the shell.

Jackie Gleason himself, in presenting the album, says: 'Here again is a selection of heart songs, familiar favourites, filled with romance and recollections.' It is a perfect example of the back cover being used to inform and to set the mood while wanting the buyer to know that he is sophisticated with a desire to be informed. It obviously worked, because *Lonesome Echo*, released in 1955, was on the *Billboard* album chart for 23 weeks, peaking at number one. Again, where Gleason led the way, others followed.

The back covers of albums featuring travel destinations can also be enticingly descriptive as well as informative. For instance, the back cover of 101 Strings' travel album *Hawaiian Paradise* has the following words:

> A musical holiday in one of the most beautiful places on earth. A breathtaking sound picture of sparkling beaches caressed by gentle travel winds. The enchantment of languid nights and hula guitars under Polynesian skies. The islands of Hawaii – truly a paradise in the Pacific.

Doesn't it make you want to go there?

And In The End ...

The golden age of easy listening music was essentially orchestral. In its latter decades, as a result of the changing trends in pop music, a soft-rock format morphed into a coalescence of pop ballad, sometimes folk and country rock, and singer-songwriter compositions that came to be labelled by the music industry 'Adult Contemporary'. In 1979, *Billboard* renamed its 'Easy Listening' chart 'Adult Contemporary'. Nowadays, it is often referred to as 'Lounge' music, which, in essence, includes any slow song sung by any of the post-1970s leading pop stars. Singers like David Soul, Barry Manilow, Celine Dion, Rod Stewart, Phil Collins, Michael Buble, the late Amy Winehouse, James Blunt and probably now even Ed Sheeran. It nevertheless remains music for grown-ups who want to escape the excitable sounds of rock and rap music in all its youth-orientated rebel forms and genres.

A Note

I have not described all the tracks on all the singles, EPs and albums I have included in this study, simply because there are fundamental similarities in their arrangements. It might have become repetitive for you, the reader. What I have done, however, is demonstrated how each of the orchestra and band leaders either changed or brought something new to the genre, keeping it alive, not to mention, thrilling its devotees throughout the era.
Discographies appear at the end of each major artist's study and there is a general discography at the end of the book. There are numerous links to every conceivable kind of easy listening music on the internet. The number of orchestras that play it would fill a volume of the Encyclopaedia Britannica.

Important Artists Of The Golden Age Of Easy Listening

Paul Weston

Key Recording: Music For Dreaming

Released as a 4×Shellac, 10", 78 RPM, Album
Tracklist:
Record 1): 'I Only Have Eyes For You' (Harry Warren, Al Dubin) b/w 'So Beats My Heart For You' (Pat Ballard, Ray Henderson and Fred Waring)
Record 2): 'If I Love Again' (Jack Murray and Ben Oakland) b/w 'Rain' (Eugene Ford)
Record 3): 'You Came Along From Out Of Nowhere' (By John W. Green and Edward Heyman) b/w 'Don't Blame Me' (Dorothy Fields and Jimmy McHugh)
Record 4): 'I'm In The Mood For Love' (Jimmy McHugh) b/w 'My Blue Heaven' (Walter Donaldson and George A. Whiting)
Label: Capitol Records
Release date: 1945

Paul Weston was born on 12 March 1912. He was, in fact, born Paul Wetstein in Springfield, Massachusetts, to Paul Wetstein, a teacher, and Anna 'Annie' Grady. The family moved to Pittsfield when Weston was two, and he spent his formative years in the town. His parents were both interested in music and when Paul Sr. taught at a private girls' school, he was allowed to bring the school's gramophone home over the Christmas holidays and the younger Paul remembered listening to 'Whispering Hope' being played on it.

At the age of eight, he started piano lessons. He studied economics at Dartmouth College in New Hampshire, graduating in 1933. During his college days, Weston formed his own band, calling it The Green Serenaders. Wanting to travel with the college band, he learned to play the clarinet. At Columbia University, he played in the university band, Blue Lions. In January 1934, Weston was seriously injured in a train accident. Managing to grab a door handle as the train pulled away, he was dragged two and a half miles along the track before letting go. His injuries prevented him from playing in bands, but as a way of keeping his oar in with music while convalescing, he started arranging musical scores. Returning to New York in the autumn of 1934, he sold one of his arrangements to Joe Haymes. Haymes so liked his work, he asked him to do more arrangements for his band. His medley of 'Anything Goes' songs caught the ear of Rudy Vallee, who offered him a job as an arranger for his radio show *Fleischmann's Hour*.

Weston was gaining a reputation for being an innovative arranger. Through his work with Joe Haymes, he met Tommy Dorsey. Having split from his brother in 1935, Tommy had yet to form his own orchestra and used the Joe Haymes Orchestra for his first engagement as a solo conductor. Weston joined Dorsey as chief arranger in 1936, staying with him until 1940. He was soon in demand by other artists and became Dinah Shore's arranger/conductor and worked freelance for the Bob Crosby Orchestra and Paul Whiteman. Bob Crosby was Bing Crosby's brother. Bing hired his brother's orchestra to play in his film *Holiday Inn*. Weston went with him, thus gaining him an entry into Hollywood and other film work. Changing his name from Wetstein to Weston, he was asked to create further musical scores for Bing Crosby, Bob Hope and Betty Hutton. He was also musical director for the films 'Belle of the Yukon' and' Road to Utopia'.

It was around this time that lyricist Johnny Mercer came into Paul Weston's life. Mercer, along with Buddy DeSylva and record shop chain owner Glenn E. Wallichs, was about to start Capitol Records. Mercer asked Weston to write for the new company. He wrote, arranged and produced the first piece written for the new label on 6 April 1942: Mercer's 'Strip Polka'. On 1 August of the same year, The American Federation of Musicians' strike began. It was over a dispute about paying musicians royalties. The Union barred its musicians from playing for record companies. They were, however, allowed to play for live engagements and radio shows. Many record companies stockpiled recordings of their stars, which they were able to release during the strike. However, the newly formed Capitol Records had not been going long enough to do this. Consequently, the strike brought the new company to a halt almost before it had begun. In June 1943, Johnny Mercer began a radio show, *Johnny Mercer's Music Shop*. The show was intended to be a showcase of Capitol's talent during the Musicians' strike. Mercer and Capitol recording artist Jo Stafford, hosted the program, with Weston and his orchestra providing the music. Stafford and Paul Weston had first met and fallen in love in 1938 when he was working as an arranger for Tommy Dorsey, and it was Weston who arranged for her group, The Pied Pipers, to audition with Dorsey for his radio show.

The recording ban was lifted for Capitol in October 1943 after an agreement was reached between the Musicians' Union and the record companies. Weston was then able to return to the recording studio. In 1944, he became the company's music director. When appointed, Weston was the youngest musical director for any major record company. It was around this time that he began to think about arranging music to be played on record as background music to life in the home, just as he'd done in composing and arranging film scores. Thanks to General Squire's invention of what he called Muzak, music was being heard in public places and spaces all over America. Why not create recordings that could become the soundtrack to life at home? Music that would enable people to escape the distress of daily living, without it becoming intrusive enough to get in the way of the life of the home. Music that would, in fact, add an extra dimension to life in the home at such times as dinner parties for friends and lovers. Moreover, for times when one is just at home relaxing and escaping the hustle and bustle of the world outside. Weston had also noticed that the dance music of the preceding years was giving way to slower tunes, with attention switching from the band leaders and their orchestras to solo vocalists such as Frank Sinatra and Doris Day. As he said, 'Jitterbug went out and my albums filled the gap…' And there was pointedly no vocalist to dissolve the mood with meaningful thoughts.

Music For Dreaming was Paul Weston's first album release on Capitol Records. It was issued on the 78-rpm format in an album-style box set of four 10" shellac records, as the long-playing (LP) vinyl format was not yet current. He was not entirely sure the record-buying public was ready for this new kind of music and initiated market research in ten major US cities. He need not have worried. The album became a best-seller, with sales of over 175,000 copies, a huge number for the times. It was no chance thing. Weston knew exactly what he was doing. He described his style as 'under arranged' and 'underplayed', and in adding strings to dominate what was basically the framework of a jazz band, he considered he'd set the trend for what he and the bands and orchestras that followed did in metamorphizing muzak into domestic 'mood music', as it was descriptively called at the time.

As previously mentioned, in 1950, *Coronet* magazine called him 'the master of mood music' for his 'smooth, shimmering arrangements'. Weston later declared he was the first person to whom the expression 'mood music' was applied. He unashamedly admitted his mood music albums 'walked a narrow line between respectable jazz and wallpaper music'.

Weston's stroke of genius was to rearrange tunes that the public already knew and loved. Their familiarity with these pop tunes was to align the new with the comfortable familiarity of the old. This is what distinguished Weston's music from Muzak, which was usually music anonymously composed, relatively bland and lacked any kind of musical hook to catch the listener's attention.

Reading through the tracks as described below, you can get a sense of how Weston used the orchestra to create a feeling of mood, rather than simply pleasurable listening to a song. For the most part, strings and brass take the lead, with the introduction of solo instruments – like clarinet, flute and oboe – to add character. It is this approach that adds colour to his pieces, helping to differentiate between the separate parts of each song. The introduction of the double bass and percussion into Weston's arrangements creates a rhythm section, whose job it is to supply the beating heart of the mood created. It usually consists of bass and drums, and sometimes keyboard instruments.

In this first, what can be called, easy listening album, Weston sets the trend as to what shape and size an easy listening track should take. There are twelve tracks that total 36 minutes, averaging at around three minutes per track. The three to three-and-a-half-minute song became an accepted standard in easy listening recordings, as it had in the pop world, mainly to suit radio station programming formats. In shaping his arrangements, it is obvious that Weston and his producer had borne this in mind. But there is also, and more importantly, the knowledge that a mood can only be sustained for so long before the magic of it begins to fade.

'I Only Have Eyes For You'

A romantic love song written for the film *Dames* (1934). It became a jazz standard and had been covered by numerous musicians, Ben Selvin having had a hit record with it in 1934. Here, vibrato strings, together with harp and tinkling piano, give a melancholic start to the song before the full string section gains the ascendency. There is something of a big band feel as the brass section enters, while the mood takes on a swooning feel. The string section drives the melody, accompanied by brass and woodwind, with the harp adding a feeling of brightness and shadow. The mood is celebratory and reassuring throughout.

'So Beats My Heart For You'

Another jazzy love song which had been a hit record for Earl Burtnett and His Los Angeles Biltmore Hotel Orchestra. The flute introduces the melody, which is then picked up by the strings and brass sections. The strings then fade into the background, allowing the brass and wind sections to again drive the melody. Peaks and valleys are provided throughout by the strings. The mood is consistently sweet and romantic, as the strings literally carry you off on gently uplifting waves of emotion.

'If I Love Again'

A swooning love song. Strings draw you in again from the start, with a harp adding a touch of lyricism. The strings and harp act like an opening verse or chorus, with an undertone from the flute adding another dimension in the background. A change from previous songs in that the woodwind section takes over the melody, sharing it between saxophone and oboe. Although the oboe is present in many of the songs on this album, this is the first time the saxophone has come to the fore. Muted trumpets are brought in to carry the song along and, supported by strings, add colour and range. The mood is contemplative and wistful, with a sense of resolve at the end to rush back to where angels have feared to tread.

'Rain'

Strings open the song, again, along with scattering notes to give an otherworldly feel, as a mixture of woodwind and brass introduce the melody, leaving the strings to fill out the sound as a jazzy piano momentarily creeps in. The woodwind section then drops back, allowing the brass section, with its sharper sound, to dominate. This is a track that makes you want to take your lover in your arms in a smoochy embrace and, with a lovesome look in your eyes, move ever so gently in a slow dance. There may be rain, but it is not a torrential downpour; rather, a soft, spring shower.

'Out Of Nowhere'

Much like the rest of the album, strings draw us into the melody. However, on this occasion, to add drama, a single clarinet introduces the beginnings of the melody. Structure is given by the brass and strings sections, with a smattering of harp to add swells and fades where needed to enhance the mood. The clarinet again picks up the melody, at the same time adding more light and shade. The mood here is light and joyous, with a sense that love will come again and from where you least expect it.

'Don't Blame Me'

Much like the previous tracks, this song is driven by strings over brass, with muted trumpets carrying the melody. There is a key change as the strings and harp enter to add contrast. This is something new in musical terms. Again, the woodwind section, primarily the clarinet, supplements the brass section to subtly give a softer descending feel to the melody. The mood is dreamily plaintive throughout.

'I'm In The Mood For Love'

Strings open the arrangement, with muted trumpets driving the melody line. There is a continuous interplay, resulting in dynamic shifts that alternate between the bold and the subtle. This track, particularly, could be used in a masterclass to demonstrate how to build and heighten the mood of a song. Its mood is quietly seductive, wanting to gently take you away from the kitchen sink and deliver you ever so gently into the arms of love.

'My Blue Heaven'

This was first sung in 1927 by Tommy Lyman as the theme music to his radio show. Weston varies the pace as the song progresses. The brass section takes the lead, while a double bass sets the pace and an oboe gives a low woodwind resonance. Strings then come in to lift the melody, with a harp adding colour throughout. The mood is playful. The lovemaking is done and now we must be glad it happened and know that it is going to happen again and forever after, no matter how dull life is in between.

Music For Dreaming continued to sell well and in 1950, Capitol re-released it on a 10" vinyl album, with added tracks, and again in 1959 on a 12" LP (Capitol ST-1154), this time re-recorded in glorious stereo, fourteen years after the original 1945 78 RPM album release. *Billboard* said of this latter release:

> Romantic, lush sound is applied by the orchestra on a lovely set of tunes. It's a soft programming package for late-hour listening. Stereo adds to the appreciation of the beautifully arranged selections. Those who like their music sweet and easy will go for this.

This sums up the album that launched a whole new genre of popular music.

Paul Weston died on 20 September 1996 in Santa Monica, California.

Further Listening:
Music For Memories (Capitol H-225) 10"
Music For Easy Listening (Capitol H-195) 10"
Music For Romancing (Capitol H-153) 10"
Music For the Fireside (Capitol H-245) 10"
Music For Reflection (Capitol H-287) 10"
Music For Dreaming (T-1154) 12"
Music By The Fireside (T-1192) 12"
Mood Music (Columbia Cl-527) 1953
Dream Time Music (Columbia Dl-528) 1953
Caribbean Cruise (Columbia Dl-572) 1954
Music For A Rainy Night (Columbia Cl-574) 1954
Melodies For A Sentimental Mood (Columbia Cl-6204)
Original Music For Easy Listening (CD Corinthian Cor102-Cd) 1987
Music For Memories/Music For Dreaming (CD Capitol Cdp 7 92091 2) 1992
Music For Dreamers (With The Norman Luboff Choir) (CD Sony Music Special Products 28578) 1997
Paul Weston And His Orchestra With The Norman Luboff Choir (Sony A28578) 1997
Caribbean Cruise Music For A Rainy Night (CD Collectables 6468) 2000
Mood Music/Dream Time Music (CD Collectables 6469) 2000

Jackie Gleason

Key Recording: Music For Lovers Only

Released as a 10" LP
Tracklist:
A-Side: 'Alone Together' (Howard Dietz, Arthur Schwartz)/'My Funny Valentine' (Lorenz Hart, Richard Rodgers)/'But Not For Me' (George, Ira Gershwin)/'Love (Your Spell Is Everywhere)' (Elsie Janis, Edmund Goulding)
B-Side: 'I'm In The Mood For Love' (Dorothy Fields, Jimmy Mchugh)/'Love Is Here To Stay' (George Gershwin, Ira Gershwin)/'I Only Have Eyes For You' (Harry Warren, Al Dubin)/'Body And Soul' (Edward Heyman, Robert Sour, Frank Eyton, Johnny Green)
Label: Capitol Records
Release date: December 1952

John Herbert Gleason was born on 26 February 1916 in Brooklyn, New York. He was a larger-than-life American actor, comedian, writer, composer and conductor known affectionately as 'The Great One'. Developing a style and characters from growing up in Brooklyn, he was known for his brash visual and verbal comedy, exemplified by his city-bus-driver character Ralph Kramden in the television series *The Honeymooners*.

He also developed The Jackie Gleason Show, which maintained high ratings from the mid-1950s through to 1970. Production of the show moved in

1964 from New York to Miami Beach, Florida, where Gleason had taken up permanent residence.

Gleason's music career took off when he created a series of staggeringly best-selling 'mood music' albums. Entrepreneurial by nature, Gleason was always on the lookout for ways of exploiting new musical trends. Despite lacking musical training and being unable to read music, he loved pop music and said that he conceived the idea of an album of 'slow dream music' as far back as 1941, 'but couldn't get anyone interested in it at the time'. He was advised by none other than his friend Bing Crosby to take his showbiz ideas and set up a company of his own to exploit them.

In 1942, Gleason was cast in the film Orchestra's Wives starring Glen Miller. He got friendly with Miller's trumpet player Bobby Hackett and expressed the hope that they might collaborate on some ideas he had for a musical venture. By January 1952, Gleason was hosting a television show *Cavalcade Of Stars*. He was offered a three-year exclusive contract by CBS, which was worth $6 million. Given something of a free hand, he saw an opportunity to follow up on his musical ambitions and he put together a 27-piece orchestra, calling it 'Music For Lovers Only'. His orchestra combined an over-size string section and Bobby Hacket's underplayed trumpet on smooth, moody arrangements of love song standards, no doubt copying what Paul Weston was doing so successfully on his own mood music albums. Lacking, as has been said, musical training, Gleason was nevertheless able to pick out themes on the piano, which he was able to communicate to his producers, Peter King and George Williams, both of whom knew their stuff musically. Gleason got what he was looking for: 'music to put its listeners in the mood for love'. He said, '…when I heard music, I could listen to the sounds in the back of the melody and hear it all…' However, there still remained one problem: he could not get a recording label interested enough to record an album of what he heard in his head. In true visionary and entrepreneurial style, he funded his first album himself.

Gleason initially approached Decca, but seeing him as a loud, clowning comedian, they didn't take him seriously as a music maker. Gleason's manager then persuaded Capitol Records – Paul Weston's label, which was doing very nicely out of his mood albums – to take him on. In exchange for promoting his new show on CBS, *The Jackie Gleason Show*, Capitol agreed to let Gleason make an album, but with an advance of just $1000. The rest of the production costs he would have to fund himself. Ever the entrepreneur, Gleason readily agreed to this. The huge advance he got from CBS meant he had the funds to do so. He knew exactly what he wanted to create, even down to the design of the album cover, which reflected the romantic, sexy mood of the whole recording package. He called the album *Music For Lovers Only*. Upon release in 1952, it sold 500,000 copies and remained on the *Billboard* Top Ten charts for 153 weeks.

Just as Paul Weston had done, Gleason chose to re-arrange pop standards. Exactly what part he played in the arranging of the tunes has always been hotly debated, even in his own day. It was the solo playing of trumpet player Bobby Hackett that distinguished the musical sound of the album. Newspaper columnist Walter Winchell, said that it set the album's 'groove on fire'. Charles Menees in the St. Louis Post-Dispatch said that it was the album's 'big attraction', adding that the album could just as easily have been called 'Bobby Hackett With Strings'. Avilda Peters called his playing 'a thrilling sound which breaks through the orchestral arrangement of strings and reeds'.

Of the production side of the album, Avilda Peters also wrote: 'Gleason doesn't over-orchestrate. He simply offers smooth, soft, candlelight mood music that appeals to both young and old'. Tom E. Danson wrote that in *Music For Lovers Only*, Gleason 'proves conclusively that he's as agile with the baton as in the humour department'. Doris E. Bynum in the Orlando Sentinel baulked at the album's name, but called its arrangements 'sheer heaven'.

But who did create the arrangements? Although the album credits him with having presented, selected, and conducted the music, it also credits Peter King and producer Richard Jones as arrangers. The widespread public belief was that Gleason had either played a lead role as arranger or was taking credit for the work of others. In interviews, Gleason maintained that his role in the production of the album really did go beyond selecting the tunes, acknowledging at the same time King's work as arranger and collaborator. Gleason may have had no formal musical training, but he could play trumpet, piano, and organ sufficiently well to convey his ideas to King. 'I pick the notes out on an organ', Gleason told the New York Daily News. 'I have a way of marking them down so King can interpret them'. Nevertheless, Gleason struggled to convey his ideas to professional musicians. King said that, despite Gleason's lack of musical education, his ability was 'a little more than musicians credit him with and a little less than the public thinks he knows'. Bobby Hackett expressed contradictory opinions about Gleason's acumen, saying on one occasion that professional musicians were 'always amazed' by him, however, cynically adding that 'his principal contribution to the recordings was that he brought the checks'. Similarly, Gordon Jenkins said Gleason's contribution to the arranging of the music consisted of 'sitting in the control room puffing a fat cigar while his arrangers do the conducting'.

However you look at it, Jackie Gleason was the man behind what became a whole series of over 40 gold and platinum-selling 'mood music' albums throughout the 1950s and 1960s, albums whose sales have not yet dried up 70 years after the series' first release. He may or may not have gotten the idea from Paul Weston's success with *Music For Dreaming*; he may or may not have dreamed up the idea of 'slow dream music' in 1941, before or about the same time Paul Weston was doing so, but it cannot be denied that he put 'mood music' centre-stage in the music industry and, in the process, made himself a very rich man, which may or may not have been his bandwagon-jumping original intention.

In describing a sample of tracks below, it is quite clear that Gleason had a firm idea in his mind of what shape and form this album should take and he did not deviate from it one iota. As with Paul Weston, the average length of a track is three to three and a half minutes. What makes Jackie Gleason different is the very deliberate arrangements of these musical moments. All songs open with strings and harp, lasting uniformly approximately a minute, followed by a trumpet solo/melody line, followed again by strings giving way to a trumpet solo around 20 seconds before the end of each track. Trumpet player, Bobby Hackett's influence can be felt throughout.

'Alone Together'

This first track of the album opens with a feeling of melancholia, driven by the string section and accompanied by a harp and walking bass. It is not until almost a minute into the song that the brass section is brought in. Again, the trumpets give a melancholy feel as they flow lazily in and around the melody, finally giving way to the strings. Hackett's trumpet solo closes out the piece.

'My Funny Valentine'

One of the most notable tracks on the album, the strings again drift into play, supported by the harp and double bass, as muted trumpets once more come to the fore, gently falling, with a loose swing-like feel, through the melody line. The mood created this time is steamily romantic, created by the interplay between the strings and brass. It finishes in much the same way as the first track, with the strings suddenly giving way to a trumpet solo, only to reassert themselves with a final flourish in the few bars before the solo ends. Your funny valentine is the cutest of chicks and you must let them know.

'But Not For Me'

This song has more of a Paul Gleason feel to it, that is, until after about a minute when a trumpet eases its way in a lazily swing-like way. Although less seductively romantic than other tracks on the album, the arrangement follows the same pattern of opening with strings, to be followed by a moody trumpet, with strings again adding emphasis and restraint throughout. The mood is one full of regret for a love you have to let go, knowing you are breaking a yearningly devoted heart: 'I'm sorry, sweetheart, but that's just the way it is'.

'I'm In The Mood For Love'

In contrast to Paul Weston's arrangement of this song, the typical opening of big strings is replaced with a sprinkling of notes as strings softly swirl in. The strings are accompanied again by bass to give that seductive, romantic feel. Whereas Weston uses muted trumpets to drive the melody line as it gives way to the woodwind section, Gleason's arrangement lets a full trumpet solo meander its way through the melody, adding further to the seductive feel. The use of the trumpet gives this version a more jazz-like feel than that of Paul Weston. True to form, the track finishes with the strings falling right back into the mix to allow Hackett's solo trumpet to soar. The seductive lover here is so confident that he only has to point loving eyes in the direction of the bedroom to make the object of his desires surrender her will to his.

'I Only Have Eyes For You'

With no surprises, the track opens with swirling strings, followed by a meandering jazz-flavoured trumpet solo, which leads the piece moodily through the song's chorus and verses. Typically, the strings add high and gentle drama, soaring before fading away altogether to allow the trumpet solo to give a big finish, its last few notes fading sleepily away. Is he a Lothario, or is he sincere? He convinces her he really is her Romeo and only longs to leap up onto that balcony to take her in his arms and smother her with kisses.

Jackie Gleason died on 24 June 1987 in Fort Lauderdale, Florida, USA.

Further Listening:

Music For Lovers Only (W 352) 1953
Music To Make You Misty (W 455) 1954
Music, Martinis And Memories (W 509) 1954
Music To Remember Her (W 570) 1955
Lonesome Echo (W 627) 1955
Music To Change Her Mind (W 632) 1956
Night Winds (DW 717) 1956
Music For The Love Hours (SW 816) 1957
0000! (SW 905) 1957
The Torch With The Blue Flame (SW 961) 1958
That Moment (SW 1147) 1958
Opiate D'amour (SW 1315) 1959
Aphrodisia (SW 1250) 1960
Love Embers And Flame (SW 1689) 1960
The Gentle Touch (SW 1519) 1961
Lover's Portfolio (SWBO 1619) 1961 [2]
Today's Romantic Hits For Lovers Only (SW 1978) 1963
Music Around The World For Lovers Only (SW 2471) 1966
The Now Sound... For Today's Lovers (SW 293) 1968
Come Saturday Morning (ST 480) 1970
Night Winds/Music To Make You Misty (CD Capitol C2-92088) 1991
Instrumental Favourites (CD Time Life Music R956-11) 1995
The Romantic Moods Of Jackie Gleason (CD Capitol 52541) [2] 1996
Tawny/Music, Martinis, And Memories (CD Collectors' Choice 168) 2000

Frank Chacksfield And His Orchestra

Key Recording: 'Ebb Tide'

Released as a 45-rpm 7" single
Label: London Records
Release date: 1953

Frank Chacksfield was born on 9 May 1914 in Battle, East Sussex, England. He did not come from a musical family, but, showing a gift for music at an early age, he was tutored on the organ by J. R. Sheath-Dare (1857-1934), while at the same time learning to play piano. He became deputy church organist at nearby Salehurst. He appeared at the Hastings Music Festival at the age of fourteen. He worked for a time in a solicitor's office but knew that what he really wanted was a career in music and the late 1930s saw him leading a small band in Tonbridge, Kent. His musical career was given a boost when, after joining the Royal Army Service Corp at the start of World War II, he was heard giving a piano recital on BBC radio and was promptly posted to ENSA, an organisation established in 1939 by Basil Dean and Leslie Henson to provide entertainment for British armed forces personnel in the various theatres of war throughout WWII. It was in ENSA that he met and worked with Charlie Chester, who was to become a famous UK broadcasting personality in the decades after the war. Chester got Chacksfield work as an arranger and conductor on BBC radio. Working as musical director for Geraldo and Henry Hall, he began making records under the name of Frank Chacksfield's Tunesmiths. In early 1953, he had a Top Ten hit with a novelty song 'Little Red Monkey' (Parlophone R.3658). This led to him signing a contract with Decca and forming his own 40-piece orchestra, which included a large string section, often called 'The Singing Strings'.

His first release for Decca, 'Terry's Theme' (London 1342, UK), was a rendition of the theme music to the Charlie Chaplin film *Limelight*. A popular tune that had been recorded by numerous other artists, Chacksfield scored a US hit with it, winning a Gold Disc and a UK number two hit. It stayed at the number two position in the UK for eight weeks (an all-time UK record) and in the top five for thirteen, winning *NME*'s prestigious Record of the Year award.

'Ebb Tide'

Chacksfield's next release was 'Ebb Tide'. It scored an even bigger success on both sides of the Atlantic and was the record that established him as an orchestra leader to rival the likes of Paul Weston, Jackie Gleason and Mantovani. It was the first British instrumental record to reach the top of the US charts, and his 'outfit' was voted the most promising new orchestra of the year.

This was originally a popular song written in 1953 by lyricist Carl Sigman and composer Robert Maxwell. It was intended to echo sea waves rising and falling on an ebb tide. Chacksfield adds to the arrangement a sensual, even sexual, feel, along with, incidentally, the sound of seagulls. He is quoted by www.spaceagepop.com as saying:

> Orchestras are more than just a combination of sounds; they are not unlike people. Orchestras have moods and feelings, and above all, they can express those feelings. The best orchestras can make you angry and sad and even fall in love.

Chacksfield used the large string section of his orchestra to enhance the seductive moodiness of his arrangement. Modern recording techniques allowed him also to experiment with layering, i.e., in recording parlance, overdubbing, which enabled him to create a lavishly rich, sweeping sound.

Frank Chacksfield went on to become one of Britain's best-known orchestra leaders, presenting shows on BBC TV and arranging the country's first Eurovision Song Contest entry in 1957 – 'All' by Patricia Bredon. He and his orchestra recorded more than 150 top-selling albums, which sold worldwide, especially in France, Germany, Australia and Japan, notching up sales of over 20 million.

In the 1960s, Dutch pirate radio station Radio Veronica, sampled Chacksfield tracks to create jingles for its news bulletins.

From the 1970s onwards, he recorded mainly on Decca's Phase 4 label, releasing a well-received album of Beatles covers (PFS 4191) in 1970. He also became actively involved with Starborne Productions, a US company created to specifically supply easy listening music, when it was felt general record stores were no longer stocking it. Initially, this was done by using what was called 'IN-WATS', a system designed by a company called Disc Location to send tracks on demand down the telephone line in much the same way as General Squier had imagined way back at the beginning of the century. Callers were greeted with a friendly:

'Hello, thank you for calling Disc Location. May I have the artist's name and the song title you're looking for?'

Chacksfield arranged and conducted much of the output of Starborne Productions, a lot of which was used, not just by US radio stations specialising in an easy listening format, but also by the BBC in the 1980s and the 1990s, before 24-hour-a-day programming arrived in the UK, to accompany Testcard screenings and the automated TV news and information service Ceefax.

Frank Chacksfield died on 9 June 1995 in Bromley, Kent, UK.

Further Listening:

Velvet (London LL-1443)
'South Sea Island Magic' (London LL-1538)
Mediterranean Moonlight (London LL-1588)

'On The Beach' (London LL-3158)
Evening In Paris (London LL-14081)
Immortal Serenades (London PS-122)
'Love Letters In The Sand' (London PS-145)
The Million Sellers (Richmond S-30045) 1960
'Ebb Tide' (Richmond 30078) 1961
The New Ebb Tide (London Phase 4 SP-44053) 1964
Ebb Tide And Other Million Sellers (London Phase 4 BSP-24) 1969
Plays The Beatles Songbook (London Phase 4 SP-44142) 1970
Plays Simon And Garfunkel And Jim Webb (London Phase 4 SP-44151) 1970
'Rise' (Excelsior XRP-7000) 1980
'After the Lovin'' (Excelsior XRP-7005) 1980
'Sunflower' (Excelsior XRP-7006) 1980
Dust In The Wind (Excelsior XRP-708) 1980
'Love Is In The Air' (Excelsior XRP-7009) 1980
Streaks Of Lavender (CD Omega W-021-2) 1993
Frank Chacksfield Vol 1 (CD Frank Chacksfield private stock FCCD-1001) 1994
Sounds Of Romance (CD Good Music Company 199927) 1998 [2]
Dinner At Eight-Thirty (CD Vocalion 4109) 2001
Thanks For The Memories (CD Polygram International 544250) 2001

Mantovani

Key Recording: Waltz Encores

Released as a Vinyl LP
Tracklist:
A-side: 'Charmaine'/'Wyoming'/'Love Makes The World Go 'Round' (La Ronde)/'Love, Here Is My Heart'/'Lovely Lady'/'The Moulin Rouge Theme'
B-side: 'Greensleeves'/'Lonely Ballerina'/'The Kiss In Your Eyes'/'Dear Love, My Love'/'I Live For You'/'Dream, Dream, Dream'
Label: Decca/London Records
Release date: 1958

Mantovani was born Annunzio Paolo in Venice, Italy, on 15 November 1905 into a musical family. His father, Benedetto Paolo 'Bismarck' Mantovani, was a violinist and served as the concertmaster of La Scala Opera House's orchestra in Milan under the baton of the great Arturo Toscanini. The family moved to England in 1912, where young Annunzio studied at Trinity College of Music in London. After graduation, he formed his own orchestra, which played in and around Birmingham. He married Winifred Moss in 1934, having two children: Kenneth (born 12 July 1935) and Paula Irene (born 11 April 1939).

Although steeped in classical music and being seen as something of a child prodigy, Mantovani decided not to follow his father into a concert career but instead to go into the world of popular band and orchestral music. Possessing charm and star quality, he quickly became popular, first at the Metropole

Hotel and later in cabaret at the Monseigneur's. By the time World War II broke out, his orchestra was one of the most popular British dance bands, both on BBC radio broadcasts and in live performances. But like so many of the great band leaders, Glen Miller being not the least of them, he was groping to find a sound that was entirely his own. He knew it had to involve strings and lots of them, but he was still not quite there in creating it. In 1951, he sought the help of Ronald Binge, who had played the accordion in his early band, The Tipica Orchestra. Binge, also a composer and arranger, had composed 'Sailing By' – still used today on BBC Radio 4 to introduce its legendary shipping forecast – a dreamy, atmospheric piece of music that has all the hallmarks of early mood music.

By now, having had hit singles across the Atlantic, Mantovani was asked by Decca Records in the US to make an album of waltzes, which resulted in *Waltz Encores*. He asked Binge to help with the arrangements. Mantovani told Binge that what he was trying to replicate in his music was the reverberating sound of religious music as it echoed around cathedrals. Binge was able to create the sound Mantovani was looking for in his arrangement of 'Charmaine'. 'Charmaine' was originally written for the silent film *What Price Glory* by composer Erno Rapee. Guy Lombardo had a number-one *Billboard* hit with his recording of it in 1927. Gordon Jenkins and His Orchestra, with Bob Carroll on vocals, had a lesser hit with it in 1951. The tune, however, had been largely forgotten until Ronald Binge resurrected it and re-arranged it for Mantovani. Binge's arrangement gave rise to what was to become known as the 'Mantovani sound': the cascading strings that flowed lushly and insistently in and around the melody. As with so much pop music of the 20th century and beyond, it could not, however, have been created without the benefit of contemporary recording techniques. (Think Joe Meek, The Beatles – although when George Martin suggested adding strings to their song 'Yesterday', Paul McCartney is reputed to have said 'I don't want to sound like Mantovani' – Pink Floyd and Brian Eno). Mantovani's recording engineer from the early days was Arthur Lilley. He used multiple microphones to create, what nowadays would be called, a 'wall of sound' (think Phil Spector) that enabled Mantovani's cascading strings to flow and echo tsunami-like in and around what were, as was normal by now in the world of mood music, the simple melodies of familiar sounding pop tunes. The recordings were made in stereo and Mantovani became the first recording artist to sell a million stereophonic records. Binge ceased arranging for Mantovani in 1952, but Mantovani had found his 'sound' and his 'cascading strings' were at the heart of everything he recorded thereafter.

Unlike Paul Weston or Jackie Gleason, Mantovani's arrangements, while still irresistibly romantic, were not, however, made with seduction as their endgame, but rather a sweet embrace.

Recording exclusively for Decca and its US arm, London, Mantovani went on to release over 50 albums, all of which were Top 40 chart hits, with many making it into the Top Ten. In 1957, his album *Film Encores* hit the number-one spot, and in 1961, he had a million-seller album with *Exodus And Other Great Themes*. He was England's highest album seller before The Beatles.

He had a UK number-one (US number-eight) hit single in 1953 with 'The Song from Moulin Rouge', also known as 'It's April Again', a pop song that was first heard in 1952 in the French film *Moulin Rouge*. Similarly, he had hit singles with 'Around the World' (US number twelve, UK number 20), the theme tune to the 1957 film *Around The World In 80 Days*, 'Swedish Rhapsody' (1953, UK number two), 'The Main Theme From Exodus ('Ari's Theme' (US number 31)), theme tune to the 1960 film *Exodus*, 'Games That Lovers Play' (1966, US number 122), and 'Theme From Villa Rides' (1968, US AC number 36).

In 1959, Mantovani also starred in his own US syndicated television series, of which there were 39 episodes, all filmed in England.

His 'sound', or, at the very least, echoes of it, can be heard in most easy listening music that followed. It could even be argued that the 'cascading' vocal harmony in The Beatles' song 'She's Leaving Home' on their 1967 album *Sgt Pepper's Lonely Hearts Club Band* is pure Mantovani. It has to be remembered that before the rock revolution of the 1950s and 1960s, easy listening music was all pervasive on BBC radio's The Home Service, the only 'pop' radio station to be heard across the United Kingdom until the pirates came along. The Kinks, in their 1980 song 'Prince Of The Punks', speak of 'A well-known groover, rock 'n' roll user', who finally makes it as a punk singer, having 'been through all of the changes/From rock opera to Mantovani'.

As will be seen below in the description of tracks sampled from *Waltz Encores*, Mantovani's invention of 'cascading' strings is the new sound never before heard in orchestral music. However, it is also the subtle, and sometimes not so subtle, use of a wide range of supporting instruments that adds to this feel of 'newness'. For example, the accordion and piccolo add depth, whereas other instruments enhance the overall sound.

'Charmaine'

From the beginning, the strings wash over you like a cataract of water gushing over a rocky precipice, immersing you in a world of romance as a muted trumpet enters and develops the melody, followed by strings to sustain this mood of unbridled romance. Then, a solo violin comes in to continue the melody whilst the remainder of the string section sits back in the mix. A bass clarinet takes the piece almost to the end before a short, muted trumpet lets the mood gently fade away. All these subtle changes across solo violin, brass and woodwind give highs and lows to the song. The mood is almost unbearably passionate, sending shivers down the spine of anyone who is not, at the precise moment, caught up in a loving embrace.

'The Moulin Rouge Theme'

Here, an accordion at the beginning takes you immediately to Paris, the city of love and romance, as swirling strings glide in to further enhance the mood. Throughout, the accordion returns to remind you of where you are, while those irresistibly pervasive strings make you want to surrender to whatever your lover passionately asks of you in this dreamscape of wine, roses and amour.

'Greensleeves'

The track opens with the feeling of courtly elegance as we picture a handsome prince reaching out to take the hand of his melting princess. From the start, Mantovani's 'cascading' strings wash over everything, as that most gently insistent of melodies (reportedly written by Henry VIII himself) wistfully carries us along. Violins give way to brass, solo violin and more swirling strings, as finally, a piccolo asks our prince to lead his love away from the dance to fall in an amorous clinch onto velvet cushions in one of the castle's candle-lit gothic recesses.

'Dream, Dream, Dream'

After a muted trumpet opening, 'cascading' strings, with a soft, muted horn playing the melody, continued by a muted French horn, wash over everything throughout. It is a dream of love and you are swept off your feet by it and taken away from the kitchen sink by a Valentino who only has eyes for you, you alone and, yes, yes, only you.

Mantovani died on 30 March 1980 at his country home in Tunbridge Wells, England.

Further Listening:

Some Enchanted Evening (London LL-766) 1953
Romantic Melodies (London LL-979) 1954
Waltz Encores (London PS-119) 1955
Film Encores (London PS-1700) 1957
Gems Forever (London PS-3032) 1958
Film Encores, Vol 2 (London PS-3117) 1959"
Continental Encores (London PS-147) 1959
The American Scene (London PS-182) 1960
Music From Exodus And Other Great Themes (PS-3231) 1961
Italia Mia (London PS-3239) 1961
American Waltzes (PS-248) 1962
Moon River And Other Great Film Themes (London PS-249) 1962
Play Selections From 'Stop The World I Want To Get Off'/'Oliver' (London PS-270) 1962
The World's Great Love Songs (London PS-280) 1962
Classical Encores (PS-269) 1963

Mantovani/Manhattan (PS-328) 1964
The Incomparable Mantovani (London PS-392) 1964
The Mantovani Sound (London PS-419) 1965
Mantovani Magic (London PS-448) 1966
Mr. Music… Mantovani (London PS-474) 1966
Mantovani/Hollywood (London PS-516) 1967
The Mantovani Touch (London PS-526) 1968
Mantovani… Memories (London PS-542) 1968
The Mantovani Scene (London PS-548) 1969
The World of Mantovani (London PS-565) 1969
Mantovani Today (London PS-572) 1970
From Monty With Love (2 LPS) (London XPS-585/6) 1971
M: Annunzio Paolo Mantovani (Twenty-fifth Anniversary Album) (London XPS-610) 1972
The Greatest Gift Is Love (London PS-913) 1975
Favourite Screen Themes (CD Pickwick PWK-128) 1991
Instrumental Favorites (CD Time Life Music R986-05) 1995

Percy Faith

Key Recordings: 'Theme From A Summer Place' and Themes For Young Lovers

Released as a 45 RPM 7" Single ('Summer Place'), Vinyl LP (Young Lovers)
Tracklist:
A-Side: 'I Will Follow You' (A. Altman, Del Roma, J.W. Stole, J. Plante, N. Gimbel)/'End Of The World' (A. Kent, S. Dee)/'Rhythm Of The Rain (J. Gummoe)/'Go Away Little Girl' (G. Goffin, C. King)/'Amy' (B. Mann, C. Weil)/'On Broadway' (M. Stoller, J. Leiber, B. Mann, C. Weil)
B-Side: 'Up On The Roof' (G. Goffin, C. King)/'Can't Get Used To Losing You' (D. Pomus, M. Shuman)/'Our Day Will Come' (Written by – B. Hilliard, M. Garson)/'All Alone Am I' (A. Altman, M. Hadjidakis, J. Ioannidis)
Label: Columbia Records
Release date: September 1959 ('Summer Place'), 1963 (Young Lovers)

Percy Faith was born in Toronto, Ontario in Canada on 7 April 1908. He was a Canadian-American bandleader, orchestrator, composer and conductor, known for his lush arrangements of pop and Christmas standards. He is often credited with popularising the 'easy listening' or 'mood music' format. He became a staple of American popular music in the 1950s and continued well into the 1960s. Though his professional orchestra-leading career began at the height of the swing era, he refined and rethought orchestration techniques, including the use of large string sections, to soften and fill out the brass-dominated popular music of the 1940s.

He was a principal player of the Canadian Broadcasting Corporation's live-music programming from 1933 to 1940. Then he moved to Chicago, where he became an orchestra leader for CBS. He also worked for Decca Records and Columbia Records, with whom he released dozens of albums: *Delicado* (1952), *Percy Faith Plays Romantic Music* (1954), *Girl Meets Boy* (1955), *Swing Low in Hi-Fi* (1956) to name but a few. At the same time, he was providing arrangements for 1950s pop singers such as Doris Day, Johnny Mathis and Tony Bennett, for whom he arranged his gold record hit 'Cold, Cold Heart', which was originally a hit for country singer legend Hank Williams. He also worked closely with Guy Mitchell, writing his 1950 hit 'My Heart Cries For You'. Faith's career had begun at the height of the swing era, but it was obvious that what turned him on was not brass orchestrations, but smooth string orchestrations – and the smoother, the better. Swing was for dancing, mood music for easy, relaxed listening where the listener was anywhere but on a dance floor. He said his goal was to 'satisfy the millions of devotees of that American institution known as the quiet evening at home, whose idea of perfect relaxation is the easy chair, slippers and good music'.

The culmination of Faith's smooth orchestrations was his 1959 arrangement of the Max Steiner and Mack Discant classic 'Theme from A Summer Place', which won him a Grammy Award for Record of the Year in 1961. It reached number one on the *Billboard* Hot 100 chart (UK number 2") and stayed there for nine consecutive weeks. Faith had taken mood music from out of the elevator, the department store, the workplace, the airport, the home, in fact, any of the places people inhabited, and put it right up there, where, as Frank Sinatra sang, it was '...Top of the list/Head of the heap/King of the hill…' In other words, easy listening orchestral music had arrived.

The piece was originally the theme music, as the title suggests, for a film. It had been arranged by Hugo Winterhalter and was rather run-of-the-mill cinematic mood music. But in Percy Faith's arrangement, the strings, most importantly, are higher up in the mix and dominate as a vocal melody would. Die-hards even said there were shades of Fats Domino in its pounding triplets. This does not happen in mood music or muzak, so something new had arrived and, importantly, people obviously liked it.

In 1963, Faith followed up the huge success of 'Theme From A Summer Place' with an equally successful album called *Theme For Young Lovers*. It was an album of pop songs given what could now be called the 'Percy Faith treatment'. The New York Times said he 'specialised in turning the simple melodic line supplied by other composers into full-scale orchestrations'. This was true and it hadn't been done before. He took pop songs like The Drifters' 'Up On The Roof' and Andy Williams' 'I Can Get Used To Losing You' and turned them into an orchestral delight of dreamily uplifting string arrangements. You heard the melody in your mind and it reminded you of how much you loved the original pop recording. Faith's arrangements also took you beyond this into a wildly romantic world of sheer pleasure that made you glad to be alive. Sad or joyous, it was just wonderful to be so moved in a way the original tunes, great though they were, had, by comparison, really only hinted at.

Though Faith initially mined the worlds of Broadway, Hollywood and Latin music for many of his top-selling 1950s recordings, from the early 1960s onwards, it was his orchestral versions of popular rock and pop hits of the day that sustained his popularity in the charts and on radio. His 1963 album *Themes For Young Lovers* (Columbia – CL2023) was a top seller, introducing his sound to a new, younger generation of listeners. With the success of Columbia record-mate Ray Conniff's chorus and orchestra during the same period, Faith, too, began using male and female choruses in his orchestrations. Released in 1967, his first single with a female chorus, 'Yellow Days' (Columbia – 44166), was a substantial hit on *Billboard*, reaching number thirteen and staying on the chart for nine weeks. It was also a radio hit on the playlists of the era's middle-of-the-road (MOR) radio stations. He received a second Grammy award in 1969 for his album *Love Theme From 'Romeo and Juliet'*. Faith continued to enjoy airplay and consistent album sales throughout the early 1970s.

Though best known for his recording career, Faith also occasionally scored motion pictures, and received an Academy Award nomination for his adaptation of the song score for the Doris Day musical feature, *Love Me Or Leave Me*. He also wrote soundtracks for romantic comedies, including *Tammy Tell Me True* (1961), *I'd Rather Be Rich* (1964), *The Third Day* (1965) and *The Oscar* (1966). He also composed the theme music for the highly successful television series *The Virginian*, which aired worldwide.

As rock music began to dominate the charts in the 1970s, Percy Faith disappeared from the pop charts, although he continued to release albums covering the music of the time with records such as *Jesus Christ Superstar* (1971 Columbia – C 31042) and *Black Magic Woman* (1972 Columbia – CQ 30800). In 1974, he released a country music album, *Country Bouquet* (1974 Columbia – KC 33142), with tunes as diverse and unlikely as 'El Paso' and 'Orange Blossom Special' being given his dazzling strings interpretation. Disco did not pass him by and in 1975, he released two dance-orientated albums: *Disco Party* (Columbia – KC 33549) and *Mucho Gusto Viva!* (Columbia – CS-10.208). His swan song, released posthumously, was a disco re-arrangement of the record that launched his easy listening career, newly entitled 'Summer Place (76)'. Released as a single on Columbia (10233), it reached number thirteen and stayed on the charts for ten weeks.

In his arrangements, as sampled below, Faith uses a simple percussive backbeat so as not to distract from the main orchestral arrangement. He does not, as might be expected, use a double bass to underpin the rhythm. Instead, using modern recording techniques, he expertly weaves the melody into his arrangements by layering the full range of the orchestra's instruments. Where other arrangers of his time might have used the strings and brass sections of the orchestra to create a bigger sound using crescendo and diminuendo, Faith does so by creating drone-like repetition, as if he has pulled the 'hook' out of the tune, putting it out there for all to hear, before suddenly letting the main melody swoop in to dominate.

'Theme From A Summer Place'

This is probably one of the most famous songs of the golden era of easy listening music. The woodwind section of the orchestra opens the track, with a backdrop of the simple metronomic percussion that became synonymous with Percy Faith's arrangements. Strings, brass and woodwind intertwine to add contrast, with the violins taking the lead role to deliver the melody, dropping back to allow the horns to take a turn. Throughout, the full breadth of tone and range of the violins leads the way. When you speak, vowels and consonants create words. When you play the violin, the bow articulates the music. Strokes can be long, short, connected, separated, smooth, accented, or even bouncy. Faith uses this to advantage: from the legato bow action, used to deliver a soothing, warm sound, with meandering notes, to the Martele action, used to lift the sound, with its larger rapid strokes, to finally, the pizzicato plucking of the strings. Not surprisingly, given his own musical training and background, Faith knew his violin and used this knowledge to create a new sound, heard to perfection in this arrangement. From the start, the strings tug at your heart, making you want to love and be loved. You have to if life is to have as much romantic meaning as this song has.

Themes For Young Lovers

'I Will Follow You'

The song opens with plucked pizzicato strings, with added percussion, specifically timbales and tambourine, and a fairly straight beat from the drummer's bass drum and snare. Throughout, the melody is driven by the violin section. In contrast to other arrangements of the time, the woodwind family, mainly flutes, give way to allow the brass section to play the melody, before allowing the violins to take over. What is different here is the playful way brass, woodwind and violins explore the melody. And you have found your love and you are never going to let him go.

'End Of The World'

Again, this track opens with percussion, this time with a simple swing beat, while the strings allow a piano to share the melody, with the strings using single notes and the piano playing chords. Mid-song, the piano drops out to allow the strings to soar. The woodwind section makes a brief appearance before the strings return to end the track, with a little help from their woodwind friends, while the piano takes a gentle bow at the end. Compared to 'I Will Follow You', there is much more musical nuance, but it is, again, Faith's mix of piano, woodwind and strings that gives structure to the arrangement. As with the previous track, it is the absence of a double bass and percussive simplicity that allows this interplay of instruments to remain in the fore. Sadly, he got away. Your lover just did not hear your pleas to stay.

'Rhythm Of The Rain'

Again, the track opens with the pizzicato strings and a simple drumbeat that remains constant throughout the entire track. There are no fills and spills here, just a gentle backbeat, that, however, at times deviates slightly from its metronomic-like timing, allowing the pizzicato strings, augmented, unusually, by cascading woodwind, to give a feel of falling rain. Soaring violins return to give intensity and subtlety before the pizzicato strings and woodwind return to continue sharing the melody. Faith's use of mixed bow strokes is heard throughout. But what the hell, there are plenty of pebbles on the seashore, even if I do feel so alone under this umbrella.

'Go Away Little Girl'

Again, the track opens with metronomic percussion, the tune's 'hook' being played by the woodwind section before violins sweep in to share the melody. The woodwind section also provides contrast, as pizzicato strings return to steal the melody. Ah, will she never leave me alone, and how can I resist her?

'Amy'

This arrangement demonstrates Faith's use of repetitive 'hook'. A flute plays for pretty much forty seconds and then re-emerges throughout. It is no secret that a good hook/riff is used to pull people into a song, making it instantly recognisable. Faith uses this time and time again in his arrangements. Here, as before, the various sections and instruments of the orchestra are mixed, as they variously play the melody, with, as you'd expect, violins taking the lead and percussion providing a backbeat. I can love again and will. Great joy, she wants me!

Percy Faith died on 9 February 1976 in Los Angeles, California, USA

Further Listening:

Plays Continental Music (CL-525) 1953
Plays Romantic Music (CL-526) 1953
Music Until Midnight (with Mitch Miller on oboe) (CL-551) 1953
Music For Her (CL-705) 1955
Passport To Romance (CL-880) 1956
Viva! The Music Of Mexico (CS-8038) 1957
The Sound Of Music (CS-8215) 1959
Bouquet (The Percy Faith Strings) (CS-8124) 1959
Bon Voyage! (Continental Souvenirs) (CS-8214) 1960
Carefree: The Music Of Percy Faith (CS-8360) 1961
Tara's Theme From 'Gone With The Wind' And Other Themes (CS-8427) 1961
Bouquet Of Love (Percy Faith Strings) (CS-8481) 1962
Exotic Strings (Percy Faith Strings) (CS-8702) 1962
Hollywood's Great Themes (CS-8583) 1962

Great Folk Themes (CS-8908) 1963
American Serenade (CS-8757) 1963
Shangri-La! (CS-8824) 1963
Themes For Young Lovers (CS-8823) 1963
More Themes For Young Lovers (CS8967) 1964
Broadway Bouquet (CS-9156) 1965
Themes For The "In" Crowd (CS-9241) 1966
Plays The Academy Award Winner (CS-9450) 1967
Today's Themes For Young Lovers (with Chorus) (CS-9504) 1967
For Those In Love (with Chorus) (CS-9610) 1968
Angel Of The Morning (Hit Themes for Young Lovers) (with Chorus) (CS-9706) 1968
Love Theme From 'Romeo And Juliet' (With Chorus) (CS-9906) 1969
Windmills Of Your Mind (CS-9835) 1969
The Beatles Album (Percy Faith Strings) (C-30097) 1970
Held Over! Today's Great Movie Themes (CS-1019) 1970
I Think I Love You (C-30502) 1971
Day By Day (KC-321627) 1972
Clair (KC-32164) 1973
My Love (KC-32380) 1973
Country Bouquet (KC-33142) 1974
Instrumental Favorites (CD Time Life Music A-23065-R986-02) 1994
The Percy Faith Treasury (CD Good Music Company A2-24270/138727) [2] 1994
Viva!: The Music Of Mexico/Exotic Strings (CD Taragon TARCD-1076) 2000
Continental Music/Romantic Music (CD Taragon TARCD-1078) 2000
Today's Themes For Young Lovers/For Those In Love (CD Collectables COL-CD-7429) 2002
Great Folk Themes/American Serenade (CD Collectables COL-CD-7479) 2002

Ray Conniff

Key Recording: 'S Wonderful!

Released as a Vinyl LP
Tracklist:
Side A: ''S Wonderful' (George Gershwin, Ira Gershwin)/'Dancing In The Dark' (Arthur Schwartz, Howard Dietz)/'Speak Low' (Kurt Weill, Ogden Nash)/'Wagon Wheels' (Billy Hill, Peter de Rose)/'Sentimental Journey' (Les Brown, Ben Homer, Bud Green)
Side B: 'Begin The Beguine' (Cole Porter)/'September Song' (Kurt Weill, Maxwell Anderson)/'I Get A Kick Out Of You' (Cole Porter)/'Stardust' (Hoagy Carmichael, Mitchell Parish)/'I'm An Old Cowhand (From The Rio Grande)' (Johnny Mercer)/'Sometimes I'm Happy' (Vincent Youmans, Irving Caesar)/'That Old Black Magic' (Harold Arlen, Johnny Mercer)
Label: Columbia Records
Release date: 1956

Joseph Raymond Conniff was born on 6 November 1916 in Attleboro, Massachusetts, USA. He got his musical education from his father, who taught him to play the trombone. Joining the Navy in WW11, he served under Walter Schumann, an American Grammy Award-winning composer for film, television, and theatre. After being demobbed, he joined Artie Shaw's big band, for whom he became musical arranger. In 1954, he was taken on by Mitch Miller, who was head of A&R at Columbia Records, as the label's home arranger. He worked with a number of Columbia's top recording artists, helping to create many of their biggest hits. These included:

Rosemary Clooney – 'Pet Me, Poppa' (7", 45 RPM Columbia 4-40579, 1955)
Frankie Laine – 'Moonlight Gambler' (7", 45 RPM Columbia 4-40780, 1956)
Johnnie Ray – 'Just Walkin' In the Rain' (Columbia 4-40729, 1956)
'Yes, Tonight Josephine' (7", 45 RPM Columbia 4-40893, 1957)
Johnny Mathis – 'Chances Are' (7", 45 RPM Columbia 4-40993, 1957)
'It's Not For Me To Say' (7", 45 RPM Columbia, 4-40851, 1957)
Marty Robbins – 'A White Sport Coat' (7", 45 RPM Columbia 4-40864, 1957)
'The Hanging Tree' (7", RPM Columbia 4-41325, 1959)
Frankie Laine and Johnnie Ray (Duet) – 'Up Above My Head' (7", RPM Columbia 40976, 1959)

Conniff's own first album was *'S Wonderful*, issued by Columbia in 1957. Into his orchestral arrangements of, again, as was standard by now in easy-records, pop standards, he introduced the sound of singing. Not with a singer as the lead vocal backed by an orchestra, but with the human voice being turned into 'a natural echo', a 'chorus invisible', a 'ghost' of a sound that embellished and enhanced the original.

While Mantovani had talked of wanting to create 'an effect of overlapping sound' as though his orchestra was 'playing in a cathedral', he had not taken the voices of Gregorian chant and introduced them into popular music. Ray Conniff did just that. It was while working with Mitch Mitchell that Conniff brought into being a sound he'd been struggling to give birth to. He later said:

> I was recording an album with Mitch Miller – we had a big band and a small choir. I decided to have the choir sing along with the big band using wordless lyrics. The women were doubled with the trumpets and the men were doubled with the trombones. In the booth, Mitch was totally surprised and excited at how well it worked.

Miller allowed Conniff to start making his own recordings with the arrangements of voice and orchestra he'd invented. He had limited success with single 45s and it wasn't until Columbia realised that his sound lent itself more to albums than singles that he became truly successful.

'S Wonderful! was a collection of standards that were recorded with an orchestra and what was by now his wordless singing chorus, which was made up of four men and four women. Conniff had dispensed with the usual lush string arrangements of the genre. In their place were the more brash sounds of the horns and woodwind sections of the orchestra doubled with vivacious, but still measured rather than jazzy, voices simply singing dah-de-dahs and do-de-doos along with the melody. Something new had been added to the sound of easy listening music, giving it a whole new dimension of pop music sound, which became hugely popular with the record-buying public. Conniff had struck easy listening gold and more albums followed.

The 'singers' were a hugely popular part of Ray Conniff's success and in 1959, he created 'The Ray Conniff Singers', which consisted of 12 men and 12 women, who were now no longer just 'ahing' and 'ohing', but were singing the lyrics, again to favourite pop standards. In the same year, the album *It's The Talk Of The Town* (Columbia CS 8143), was released. Also released was Conniff's hit album, *Christmas With Conniff* (Columbia CS 8185, 1959), which has remained popular to this day, winning a platinum disc for album and CD sales in 2006, 47 years after it was released.

In 1966, *Somewhere My Love* (Columbia CL2519, 1966) was released, and it brought Conniff his biggest-selling album on both sides of the Atlantic. It went platinum and won a Grammy. The title track was the theme music ('Lara's Theme') to the 1965 Oscar-winning film *Doctor Zhivago*. With lyrics added, it gave Conniff and His Singers a number-one *Billboard* single, which remained on the chart for 18 weeks. Both the single and the album also hit the charts high in Australia, Germany and Japan.

In 1970, Conniff released *Bridge Over Troubled Water* (Columbia CS 1022), an album which included Conniff's own composition, 'Someone', and re-arrangements of hits including 'I'll Never Fall in Love Again', 'Everybody's Talking' and 'Something'. It reached number 47 on the *Billboard* album chart.

In sampling the tracks below from *'S Wonderful!*, it can be seen that Conniff has replaced the conventional orchestral strings with the human voice to create a sense of fullness and contrast. The album has something of a big band feel, which is not surprising given Conniff's early career with big bands. This vocal arrangement serves a role similar to that of strings in earlier easy listening compositions. Conniff cleverly uses dropouts, key changes and his vocal choruses to make you feel as if you are being taken on a musical journey down a road that has not been trodden before.

''S Wonderful'

The track opens with trombones, quickly followed by the 'wordless' choir singing short and punchy da's before launching into the melody. This is followed by what can only be described as a question and answer between chorus and brass, particularly a trombone. As the song further progresses, the harmonies associated with the vocals' do's and da's give way to Gregorian chant, allowing the brass, led by a saxophone (a woodwind instrument, technically), to soar Mantovani-like, as they and the chorus charge towards a thrillingly dynamic crescendo to end the track. Romance here is less seductive and more celebratory, less private and more publicly on display.

'Dancing In The Dark'

This track starts with a brushed snare-drum beat, leading into beautiful choral harmonies, while the orchestra sounds, again, more like a big band, with the brass section dominating. The use of vocals and brass to determine the different points of the song is expertly performed, supported, as in the first track, by a swing feel from the percussion and walking double bass. The 'wordless' chorus dominates before the brass section swoops in and the rhythm section brings it to an altogether tight finish. Again, the overall feel of the track is of romantic celebration that is nevertheless private and intimate.

'Speak Low'

The rhythm section dominates from the start, with the bass and percussion section underpinning the choral harmonies as they make their entrance swirling like strings over the brass section. Again, there is this feel of a big band. The vocal chorus continues to function in the way strings normally do in a conventional easy listening arrangement. The brass and a chorus full of elation come together for a big ending that fades to a deep and sexy sigh. There is a plaintive feel throughout that is suggestive of a love that is rekindling after an estrangement.

'Wagon Wheels'

The title is a giveaway as we ride in a covered wagon along a singing cowboy trail. The chorus sings over a walking bass and a percussive accompaniment. The brass section begins to overlay all, adding a western swing big band flavouring. All the way through, it is the vocal that adds the highs and lows, supported by a soloing brass section. Again, the arrangement builds and builds to what you think is going to be the end, but suddenly, we are in a world full of harmonic do's and da's for 20/30 seconds, lower in the mix than before, as the full brass section dominates only to give way to a single trumpet (or is it a horn?) and percussion to complete a very tight finish with timpani and gong right at the very end. Here, a handsome cowpoke is courting a lovely cowgal; in the end, sweeping her off her feet to lie her down in the cool shade of a cotton tree by an East Texas cattle ranch barn where no one can see them.

'Sentimental Journey'

This song has a lovely swing opening delivered by the staccato playing of a guitar, double bass, percussion and the soothing lower resonance of a tuba as the chorus comes in with the woodwind section of the orchestra. This gives quite a sombre opening to the song until it suddenly breaks into full brass and an uplifting female chorus. In the first minutes of this song, Conniff has taken us on the journey suggested by the title, lifting us emotionally only to gently bring us back again with what is called in modern music parlance, a 'drop' (a lowering in volume, or ceasing altogether, of some or most instruments), before raising us up again with ascending vocals and a splash of brass. If that wasn't enough, around 40 seconds from the end, Conniff drops a key, only to climb slowly up to a new key, driven, as is to be expected by now in a Conniff arrangement, by chorus and brass. Here, the mood is one of nostalgia, with a lovingly devoted couple looking back over their time together and remembering the highs and the lows, but particularly the highs.

'Begin The Beguine'
(Mine and my mother's favourite tune above all others).
Here, it opens with quick stabs from the chorus amidst a swinging big brass feel. The female vocal expertly mimics the brass, while the male vocal adds a string-like feel to fill out the sound, as they start to sing the melody. Then, the chorus is suddenly pushed aside by a big brass interlude that sounds, for a moment, just like Artie Shaw's original arrangement of the piece. However, the chorus comes soaring in again, as you might expect strings to. The male vocals take up the melody again, with the female chorus stabbing away as it did at the start. Then brass rushes in, again to take over the melody, as the chorus starts to build in both volume and range, with the brass section now hitting us with stabs of sound, while the female chorus, like a sisterhood of angels, continues to soar heavenwards to bring the piece to a climactic end. The mood here is one of lovemaking at its most ecstatically sublime. It is wild and passionately sexy, as the couple, completely in step with one another, climax at exactly the same time.

Ray Conniff died on 12 October 2002 in San Diego, California, USA

Further Listening:
All on Columbia
'S Wonderful (CL-925) 1957
'S Marvelous (CS-8037) 1958
'S Awful Nice (CS-8001) 1958
Concert In Rhythm (CS-8022) 1958
Hollywood In Rhythm (CS-8117) 1959
Broadway In Rhythm (CS-8064) 1960
Concert In Rhythm Vol. II (CS-8212) 1960
Say It With Music (CS-8282) 1960
Memories Are Made Of This (CS-8374) 1961
'S Continental (CS-8576) 1962
Rhapsody In Rhythm (CS-8678) 1962
The Happy Beat (CS-8749) 1963

You Make Me Feel So Young (CS-8918) 1964
Friendly Persuasion (CS-9010) 1965
World Of Hits (CS-9300) 1967
Great Contemporary Instrumental Hits (C-30755) 1971
Theme From S.W.A.T. And Other TV Themes 1976
Supersónico (DIL 10363) 1984 (European release)
The 30th Anniversary Album (dil-10464) (Brazil release) 1986
Songs From The Big And Small Screen (CD 53197) 1993
40th Anniversary (CD 752274/2-460545) 1996
Concert In Rhythm (CS 8117 1959)

Ray Conniff Singers:
It's The Talk Of The Town (Columbia CS-8143) 1959
Young At Heart (Columbia CS-8281) 1960
Somebody Loves Me (CS-1642) 1961
Love Affair (CS-9152) 1965
Happiness Is (CS-9261) 1966
Somewhere My Love (CS-9319) 1966
Hawaiian Album (CS-9647) 1968
Honey (CS-9661) 1968
I Love How You Love Me (CS-9777) 1969
Jean (CS-9920) 1970
Love Story (CS-30498) 1971 (contains a Gregorian Cocktail version of 'If You Could Read My Mind')
I'd Like To Teach The World To Sing (CS-31220) 1972
Plays The Carpenters (CBS/Sony SOPM-129) 1974
Laughter In The Rain (KC-33332) 1974
Love Will Keep Us Together (KC-33884) 1975
Plays The Bee Gees And Other Great Hits (JC-35659) 1978

Lawrence Welk

Key Recording: Lawrence Welk And His Sparkling Strings

Released as a Vinyl LP
Tracklist:
Side A: 'Sunrise Serenade' (Frankie Carle, Jack Lawrence)/'Twilight Time In Tennessee' (Jay Milton, Ricky Edwards)/'Autumn Nocturne' (Josef Myrow, Kim Gannon)/'Moonlight Cocktail' (Lucky Roberts, Kim Gannon)/'Jeannine (I Dream Of Lilac Time)' (Nathaniel Shilkret, L. Wolfe Gilbert)/'Stars In My Eyes' (Dorothy Fields, Fritz Kreisler)
Side B: 'The Waltz You Saved For Me' (Emil Flindt, Gus Kahn, Wayne King)/'The Champagne Waltz' (Ben Oakland, Con Conrad, Milton Drake)/'When The Organ Played At Twilight' (Jimmy Campbell, Raymond Wallace, Reg Connelly)/'A Blues Serenade' (Frank Signorelli, Mitchell Parish)/'Twilight Time' (A. Nevins, A. Dunn, B. Ram, M. Nevins)/'Musette' (Richard Barr)

Label: Coral
Release date: 1956

Lawrence Welk was born on 11 March 1903 in Strasburg, North Dakota. His family hailed from Odessa, immigrating from Russia in 1982, and he was one of eight children. Welk left school during the fourth grade to work full-time on the family farm. Charismatic, he was possessed of a natural talent, and as a young boy, music became his life. He persuaded his father to buy him an accordion from a mail-order catalogue and he soon mastered it. He decided very early on he was going to make a career in music but promised his father that he would work on the farm until he was 21.

Throughout the 1920s, Welk performed with various bands before deciding to put together his own orchestra. He led big bands in North Dakota and South Dakota, including The Hotsy Totsy Boys and The Honolulu Fruit Gum Orchestra, before his own orchestra became the house band of a popular radio show on WNAX in Yankton, South Dakota. He began to make a name for himself, starting a daily radio show that ran from 1927 to 1936, which led to plenty of well-paying jobs for his band all over the Midwest of America.

During the 1930s, Welk led a travelling big band that specialised in dance tunes and what was then called 'sweet' music, as opposed to the hot jazz bands of performers like Benny Goodman and Duke Ellington. At first, they travelled around the country by car and, unable to afford hotel accommodation, they usually lived out of their cars. During a gig at the William Penn Hotel in Pittsburgh, an enthusiastic dancer described Welk's big band sound as 'light and bubbly as champagne'. The description struck a chord with Welk and he soon realised it would be a great tagline for advertising his orchestra, whose arrangements of popular songs were light and rhythmic while emphasising the melody and keeping a steady dancing beat.

Soon, he was performing all over the country, and in the early 1940s, started a ten-year residency at the Trianon Ballroom in London, where they regularly attracted thousands of people. By the late 1940s, he was playing at the Roosevelt Hotel in New York City. In 1944 and 1945, his orchestra featured in ten of what were called 'Soundies'. These were three-minute musical films that are now considered to be forerunners of today's music videos.

It wasn't long before television called. By now, Welk's orchestra had been named, not surprisingly, The Lawrence Welk Champagne Music Makers. It performed first on regional TV stations, but in 1955, went nationwide on ABC-TV with what was called simply The Lawrence Welk Show, which ran until 1982. The orchestra's instrumental virtuosity and Lawrence's infectious enthusiasm proved a winning combination and Welk's music, by now a blend of pop and polka, had become both familiar and captivating. The orchestra's instrumental virtuosity and Lawrence's infectious enthusiasm made the show an instant success.

Left: To paraphrase John Lennon: 'Before General Squier, there was nothing…' (*Alamy*)

Below: General Squier's dream machine. (*Red Bull Music Academy Daily*)

Left: Paul Weston: After General Squier came Paul Weston, who set the benchmark and made easy listening music different from big band jazz. (*Getty Images*)

Left: Reliably, easy listening's first commercial recording: Paul Weston's 78 RPM box set *Music For Dreaming*. (*Capitol*)

Right: The first man to 'package' easy listening music as a commodity, thereby becoming very, very rich: Jackie Gleason presents *Music For Lovers Only*. (*Capitol*)

Left: The First British Invasion: Frank Chacksfield topped the US charts with 'Ebb Tide'. (*Richmond, London Records*)

Right: The 'Elvis' of easy listening and cool personified, with his 'cascading strings'. *Waltz Encores* by Mantovani. (*London*)

Left: 'While Elvis exploded onto the world stage, Percy Faith and His Orchestra kind of waltzed onto it...' *Themes For Young Lovers*. (*Columbia*)

Right: The man who invented '... a natural echo' and a 'chorus invisible...', and wonderful it was! *'S Wonderful* by Ray Conniff. (*Columbia*)

Left: Champagne was never so bubbly! Nor easy listening! *Lawrence Welk And His Sparkling Strings* by Lawrence Welk. (*Coral, Decca*)

Right: Chet Atkins' 'Nashville Sound' gets a look-in, sans fiddles and steel guitars, with Floyd Cramer's silky stride piano. *Last Date*. (*RCA Victor*)

Left: Jazz meets classical. Its emperor was Peter Nero. *Hail The Conquering Nero*. (*RCA Victor*)

Right: Side-saddling Russ Conway morphs from a pub pounder into an easy listening tinkler. *The New Side Of Russ Conway*. (*CMS*)

Left: Another classicist who couldn't resist the call of easy listening. *The Plush Piano of Winifred Atwell* **by Winifred Atwell**. (*Blue Pie Records*)

Right: Fireworks, as easy listening's piano double act sparkle onstage. *The World's Greatest Themes* by Ferrante and Teicher. (*UA Records*)

Left: Easy listening music mogul extraordinaire – Jackie Gleeson. (*The Everett Collection*)

Right: The man who made the sound of squawking seagulls melodious – Frank Chacksfield.

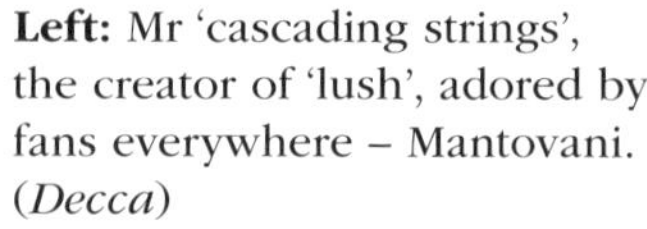

Left: Mr 'cascading strings', the creator of 'lush', adored by fans everywhere – Mantovani. (*Decca*)

Right: Summer could not have been more romantic – Percy Faith. (*Getty Images*)

Left: Ray Conniff.

Right: No band leader effervesced like him – Lawrence Welk. (*Alamy*)

Left: Nashville session man and easy listening hitmaker in his own right – Floyd Cramer. (*Country Music Hall Of Fame*)

Right: The last of the clean-cut – Peter Nero. (*Getty Images*)

Left: Russ Conway. (*russ-conway.co.uk*)

Right: The multi-talented Winifred Atwell. (*Getty Images*)

Left: Double trouble – Ferrante and Teicher. (*Getty Images*)

Right: Decca's Phase 4 Stereo techno-wizard – Ronnie Aldrich. (*Alamy*)

Left: The groundbreaking 1962 Phase 4 Stereo LP. *Melody And Percussion For Two Pianos* by Ronnie Aldrich. (*Decca*)

Right: '…the muted brass… effectively replacing the lush strings…'. *Wonderland By Night* by Bert Kaempfert. (*Decca*)

Left: Toe-tapping to all the hits. The party never ends! *Non-Stop Dancing '65* by James Last. (*Polydor*)

Right: Inspector Clouseau tripped the light fantastic to this, as Mauriat re-embraces strings. 'Love Is Blue' by Paul Mauriat. (*Phillips*)

Left: Easy listening orchestral music is nothing if it is not reprising the hits. 'Only You' by Frank Pourcel. (*Decca*)

Right: The cover says it all. *The Eyes Of Love...* by Hugo Winterhalter. (*RCA Victor*)

Left: Bert Kaempfert.

Right: Out went clean-cut white and black and in came 70s colour and bell-bottom flair – James Last. (*Gems/Redferns*)

Left: Softly, softly, love is in the air – Paul Mauriat. (*Jacques Aubert*)

Right: Frank Pourcel.

Left: Hugo Winterhalter with Eddie Fisher (left). (*Down Beat/Hip Comic*)

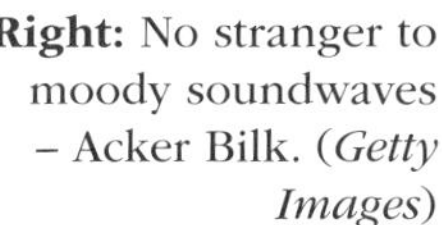

Right: No stranger to moody soundwaves – Acker Bilk. (*Getty Images*)

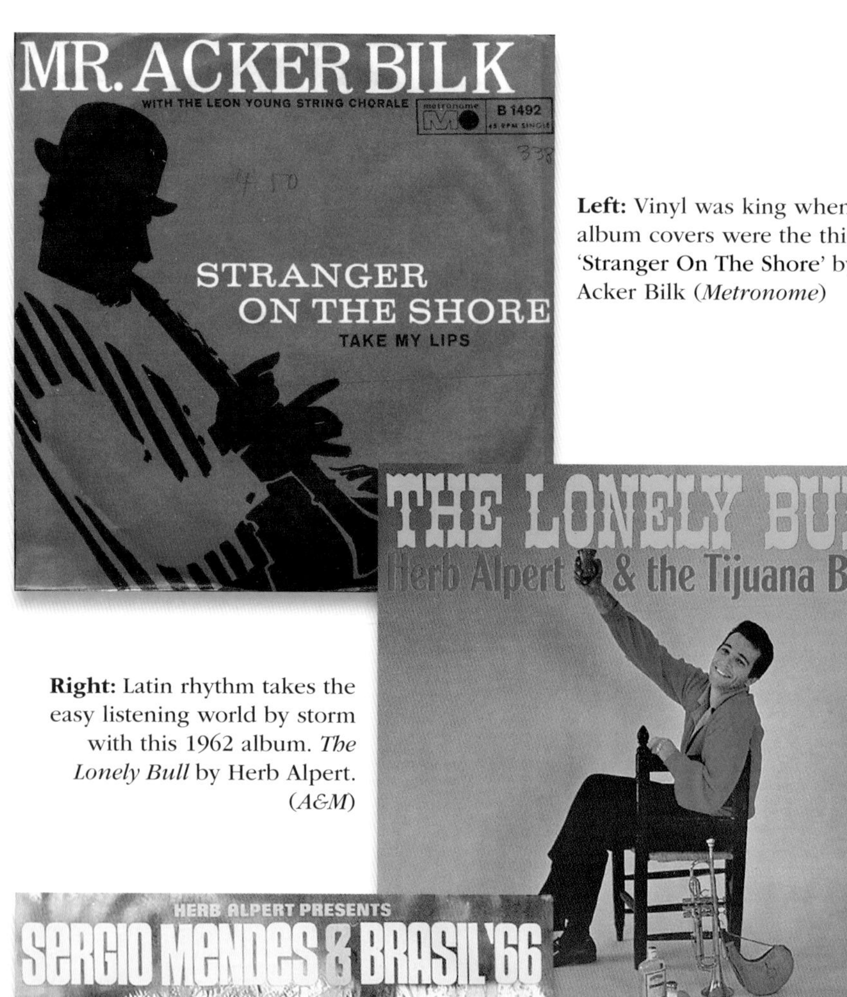

Left: Vinyl was king when album covers were the thing. 'Stranger On The Shore' by Acker Bilk (*Metronome*)

Right: Latin rhythm takes the easy listening world by storm with this 1962 album. *The Lonely Bull* by Herb Alpert. (*A&M*)

Left: When two girls replaced two pianos and took easy listening on an exotic 'Day Tripper' ride. *Herb Alpert Presents Sergio Mendez And Brazil '66* by Sergio Mendez. (*A&M*)

Right: Hollywood chic meets Huckleberry smooth. *Moon River And Breakfast At Tiffany's* by Henry Mancini. (*RCA Victor*)

Left: Heart-wrenching pathos to romantic ivory tinklings. *Love Story* by Francis Lai. (*MCA*)

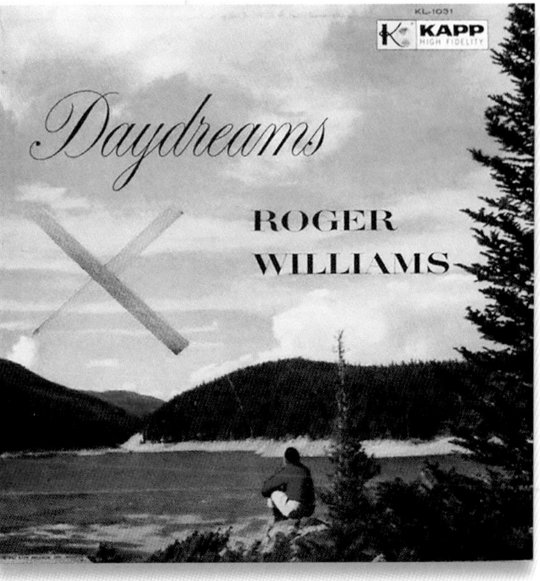

Right: Dream holidays to romantic locations for you, too. *Daydreams* by Roger Willams. (*Kapp*)

Left: Herb Alpert. (*Grandstand Media*)

Right: The man who gave it that cool, Latin beat – Sergio Mendez. (*SFJAZZ Centre*)

Left: Henri Mancini.

The whole ambience Welk and his producers created for the show was designed to imbue the viewer's evening with a sense of easy living. His charisma and genuine connection with his audience were key factors in his enduring popularity. He possessed a warm and approachable demeanour that endeared him to viewers of all ages. His catchphrase, 'Wunnerful, wunnerful', became synonymous with the joy and charm he brought to the screen, leaving an indelible impression on those who tuned in. This ability to make people feel comfortable and at ease was a crucial element of his success. A child of the times, this led Welk to very naturally fitting into what was by now our golden age of easy listening music.

Welk's TV show featured a diverse array of performers, including talented instrumentalists, vocalists and dancers, which allowed it to showcase a wide range of easy listening music, from soothing ballads to lively polkas, ensuring there was something for everyone. Welk's commitment to musical diversity was instrumental in broadening the appeal of easy listening, making it accessible to an even wider audience. He scored a whole series of hits on both *Billboard*'s singles and albums charts. It cannot be said that his music was in any way innovative and new, but his masterful adaptation of easy listening styles and arrangements of the big hitters of the day led him to produce the harmonious melodies and catchy rhythms so beloved by easy listening music fans then and now. His chart-topping hits have already been mentioned in the Overview section above.

'The Champagne Waltz'

This bubbly arrangement exemplifies Welk's signature approach to creating easy listening music. The song opens with a flurry of trills from a flute. A further sprinkling of notes adds a funday-out-at-the-fair touch, while a harmonious blend of woodwind and brass introduces the captivating melody. This contributes to the overall richness of the sound, with the appearance of a jaunty accordion for added flair.

As the composition unfolds, the woodwind section gracefully steps back, yielding the spotlight to the sharper tones of the brass instruments. Now for the fizziness of champagne bubbles as a Wurlitzer organ waltzes in.

In summary, 'The Champagne Waltz' encapsulates Lawrence Welk's hallmark style, offering a cheerful and effervescent rendition of easy listening music that's perfect for those seeking a delightful and heartwarming musical escape.

Lawrence Welk died on 17 May 1992 in Santa Monica, California, USA.

Further Listening:

Lawrence Welk And His Sparkling Strings (Coral 57011) 1956
Moments To Remember (Coral 57068) 1956
I'm Forever Blowing Bubbles (Dot DLP-25248) 1960
Songs Of The Islands (Dot DLP-25251) 1960

Last Date (Dot DLP-25350) 1961
Calcutta! (Dot DLP-25359) 1961
Yellow Bird (Dot DLP-25389) 1961
Young World (Dot DLP-25428) 1962
Baby Elephant Walk And Theme From The Brothers Grimm (Dot DLP-3457) 1962
Bubbles In The Wine (Dot DLP-25489) 1962
1963's Early Hits (Dot DLP-25510) 1963
Scarlett O'Hara (Dot DLP-25528) 1963
Wonderful! Wonderful! (Dot DLP-25552) 1964
Early Hits Of 1964 (Dot DLP-25572) 1964
My First Of 1965 (Dot DLP-25616) 1965
Apples And Bananas (Dot DLP-25629) 1965
Today's Great Hits (Dot DLP-25663) 1966
Champagne On Broadway (Dot DLP-25688) 1966
Winchester Cathedral (Dot DLP-25774) 1967
Lawrence Welk's "Hits Of Our Time" (Dot DLP-25790) 1967
Love Is Blue (Ranwood RLP-8003) 1968
Memories (Ranwood R-8044) 1969
Galveston (Ranwood R-8049) 1969
Jean (Ranwood R-8060) 1969
22 Great Songs For Easy Listening (Ranwood RLP-7016) 1982
16 Most Requested Songs (CD Columbia Legacy CK-45030) 1989
Instrumental Favorites (CD Time Life Music R986-14) 1995

Floyd Cramer

Key Recording: Last Date

Released as a Vinyl LP
Tracklist:
A-Side: 'Last Date' (Floyd Cramer)/'I Need You Now' (Al Jacobs, Jamie Crane)/'Moments To Remember' (Robert Alan)/'Tennessee Waltz' (Pee Wee King, Redd Stewart)/'Too Young' (Sidney Lippman)/'Mood Indigo' (Berny Bigard, Duke Ellington, Irving Mills)
B-Side: 'Sweetie Baby' (Lorene Rose)/'Mumble Jumble' (Floyd Cramer, Fred Bridges, Lee Williams)/'Flip, Flop And Bop' (Floyd Cramer)/'Fancy Pants' (Floyd Cramer)/'Rumpus' (Shurelon Joines)/'Heart And Soul' (Hoagy Carmichael)
Label: RCA
Release date: 1960

Floyd Cramer was born in Samti, Louisiana on 7 November 1933. He was a Nashville session pianist. Surprisingly, country music found a way into the world of what radio stations were soon to dub 'beautiful music'. Chet Atkins at RCA had invented a new, smoother sound in country music. It came to be called the 'Nashville Sound'. Rock 'n' roll had severely dented the record sales of honky-tonk music, the dominant style of country music throughout the 1950s. The 'Nashville Sound' was created to appeal to the older and now more urbanised country music fan. Like easy listening orchestral music, it used smooth strings and choruses, dispensing with fiddles and steel guitars. Floyd Cramer was Chet Atkins' primary pianist. Imitating the note-bending sound of a steel guitar, he developed the 'slip-note' (aka 'half-step' or 'bent note') style of piano playing in which a passing note slides almost instantly into or away from a chordal note, creating a sound that still, however, retained what he called 'a kind of lonesome cowboy sound'. With added strings and wordless chorus, his self-composed single, 'Last Date' (RCA Victor, 47-77750), released in 1960, was a huge hit around the world, reaching number one on the *Billboard* chart and selling over a million copies. His follow-up single, 'On The Rebound'(RCA – 45-RCA 1231), reached number one in the UK charts. Taking each year's top country and pop hits, he went on to record dozens of albums which were loved by easy listening country and pop music fans alike around the world. His sound did not have big orchestral backing and inclined more to rock 'n' roll than jazz, but nevertheless, it had all the easy listening characteristics of being non-intrusive and mood-creating. His sound became so popular that he was able to cease being a session museum and became a recording and touring star in his own right.

'Last Date'

This is an iconic instrumental piano piece. It is a shining easy listening example of the Nashville Sound, a subgenre of country music that incorporated elements of pop and smooth tempos. At its heart is Cramer's distinctive piano style, characterised by the 'slip note' technique. This technique involves playing a note, followed by sliding or 'slipping' to an adjacent note, creating a distinctive and emotionally evocative sound. Cramer's smooth and flowing piano performance perfectly captures the essence of the piece, eliciting a sense of nostalgia and longing.

The song's title suggests a sense of finality and farewell, and this sentiment is beautifully conveyed through Cramer's delicate and heartfelt piano melodies. The piece is known for its simplicity, relying on a straightforward and memorable melody that tugs at the heartstrings without the need for lyrics.

'Last Date' has transcended its era, becoming a timeless classic that resonates with audiences of all generations. It remains a beloved staple in the world of instrumental music and continues to evoke emotions and memories, making it a cherished gem in the realm of country and easy listening music. Floyd Cramer's masterpiece is a testament to the enduring power of instrumental music in touching the soul and leaving a lasting impression.

Floyd Cramer died on 31 December 1997 in Nashville, Tennessee, USA.

Further Listening:
Last Date (RCA LSP-2350) 1960
America's Best-Selling Pianist (RCA LSP-2466) 1962
Country Piano City Strings (RCA 2800) 1964
Class Of '65 (RCA LSP-3405) 1965
Class Of '66 (RCA LSP-3650) 1966
Here's What's Happening! (RCA LSP-3746) 1967
Plays The Monkees (RCA LSP-3811) 1967
Class Of '67 (RCA 3827) 1967
Class Of '68 (RCA LSP-4025) 1968
Floyd Cramer Plays Macarthur Park (RCA LSP-4070) 1969
Class Of '69 (RCA 4162) 1969
Class Of '70 (RCA LSP-4437) 1970
Almost Persuaded (RCA 2508) 1971
Class Of '71 (RCA LSP-4590) 1971
Class Of '72 (RCA LSP-4773) 1971
Class Of '73 (RCA 0299) 1973
Plays The Big Hits (RCA Camden Adl2-0128) [2] 1973
Young And The Restless (RCA 0469) 1974
Class Of '74 And '75 (RCA Apd1-1191) 1974
The Essential Floyd Cramer (CD RCA 66591) 1995

Peter Nero

Key Recording: Piano Forte

Released as a Vinyl LP
Tracklist:
A-Side: 'I Can't Get Started' (Ira Gershwin, Vernon Duke)/'Over The Rainbow' (E. Y. Harburg, Harold Arlen)/'Get Me To The Church On Time' (Alan Jay Lerner-Frederick Loewe)/'My Funny Valentine' (Richard Rodgers-Lorenz Hart)/'Scratch My Bach' (Peter Nero)/'In Other Words (Fly Me To The Moon)' (Bart Howard)
B-Side: 'Spring Is Here' (Richard Rodgers-Lorenz Hart)/'Night And Day' (Cole Porter)/'That's All' (Bob Haymes)/'Surrey With The Fringe On Top' (Richard Rodgers-Oscar Hammerstein II)/'I've Grown Accustomed To Her Face' (Alan Jay Lerner-Frederick Loewe)/'Cherokee' (Ray Noble)
Label: RCA
Release date: 1961

Key Recording: Hail The Conquering Nero

Released as a Vinyl LP
Tracklist:
A-Side: 'Midnight In Moscow' (V. Solovyov)/'When The World Was Young' (Johnny Mercer)/'My Bonnie Lies Over The Ocean' (Traditional, arranged by Peter Nero)/'What Kind Of Fool Am I?' (From Stop The World, I Want To Get Off) (Anthony Newley, Leslie Bricusse)/'Continental Holiday' (Peter

Nero)/'Granada' (Agustin Lara)
B-Side: 'Never On Sunday' (Manos Hadjidakis)/'Londonderry Air' (Traditional, arranged by Peter Nero)/'Anna' (Francesco Giordano, Roman Vatro)/'Strange Music' (George Forrest, Robert Craig Wright)/'Gloomy Sunday' (Laszlo Javor)/'Mack The Knife' (From The Three Penny Opera) (Bertolt Brecht, Kurt Weill)
Label: RCA
Release date: 1963

Peter Nero was born Bernard Nierow in Brooklyn, New York, on 22 May 1934. He started his formal music training at the age of seven. He studied piano under Frederick Bried. By the time he was 14, he was attending New York City's High School of Music & Art and had won a scholarship to the Juilliard School of Music. By the time he was 18, he'd grown tired of the rigours of classical music training and began to look towards jazz for relief, particularly Art Tatum and Oscar Peterson. After completing his graduate studies at Brooklyn College and graduating with a BA, he decided to become a jazz pianist, 'much' he says, 'to the bewilderment, chagrin and pain of everyone around me'. He did not, however, leave classical music totally behind him but created a kind of hybrid of the two, which resulted in his acclaimed jazz/classical fusion piece, 'Scratch My Bach' (track five on the album *Piano Forte* above), a wonderful piece of syncopated Baroque.

Classical/jazz fusion is not to everyone's liking and Nero did not find audiences flocking to his saloon club performances, mainly in Hickory House in New York City. However, luckily for him, Stan Geerson, a record manager at RCA (he was fellow pianist, Roger Williams' record manager at the label), heard him playing at a 'musicians' hangout' in 52nd Street and knew he could make something of him. Easy listening was where Nero's future lay, Geerson was able to persuade Nero. A name change from Barnard to Peter followed, along with a first album on RCA in 1961, *Piano Forte* (RCA LSP-2334). It was an instant success and turned Peter Nero into a nationwide sensation. His biggest-selling album was released two years later, *Hail The Conquering Nero* (RCA LSP-2638).

He had a *Billboard* Singles Chart number six hit in 1971 (13 weeks on the chart) with 'Theme From Summer of '42' (Columbia 45399) from the film of the same name. In 1971, he reached number 30 with 'Brian's Song' (Columbia 45544), a TV movie theme, and in 1975, he had number 37 hit (Arista 0112) with the theme from the soft porn film sensation, *Emmanuelle*.

Peter Nero never quite got away from his classical music roots, his music often falling between the two stools of pop and classical music. He was the founding music director of the Philly Pops (Philadelphia Pops Orchestra), which he led from 1979 to 2013. Sidney Fields in the *New York Daily News* said 'that when he [Nero] plays... jazz, people say he's too classical… and when he conducts a symphony orchestra, he's too jazzy…' But this was perhaps Nero's great appeal to easy-listing fans: they could feel cultured while at the same time being thrilled by re-invented pop melodies. From 1990 to 1999, he was also Pops Music Director of the Florida Philharmonic Orchestra, conducting and performing with his jazz trio throughout South-eastern Florida.

'I Can't Get Started'

'I Can't Get Started' commences with a dramatic burst of brass and strings. The strings create a captivating and ethereal introduction, casting an enchanting spell that transports the listener to a world beyond the ordinary.

In a harmonious dance, a blend of woodwind and brass instruments enters the scene, gracefully introducing the melody. The strings continue to weave their magic, adding depth and richness to the overall composition. As the musical narrative unfolds, a jazzy piano makes a delightful appearance, injecting a sense of whimsy and playfulness into the arrangement. The woodwind section then gracefully takes a step back, yielding the spotlight to the strings with their distinct, lush tones. The brass section emerges briefly, then yields to an emotional crescendo of strings.

'I Can't Get Started' is a track that tugs at the heartstrings, inspiring a longing to pull your beloved close. It's the kind of composition that beckons for an intimate, smoochy embrace, accompanied by a shared look of love.

Other Important Recordings

'Theme From The Summer Of '42'

This track was released in 1971 as part of the soundtrack for the film *Summer Of '42,* directed by Robert Mulligan. The film and its accompanying music are notable for their ability to encapsulate the bittersweet essence of youth and nostalgia. Nero's composition is a beautifully crafted representation of the era's popular easy listening and romantic music. It features lush orchestration and a prominent piano melody, conveying a sense of longing, innocence and melancholy. The piece is characterised by its emotive and memorable theme that evokes a feeling of wistfulness and reflection. The choice of instrumentation, including piano, strings and woodwinds, creates a rich and evocative sonic landscape, enhancing the emotional impact of the music. Nero's piano performance is particularly noteworthy, displaying his technical skill and emotional depth as a pianist. The title implies a connection to a specific time and place, which is precisely what this composition accomplishes. It captures the essence of a summer romance and the emotions associated with the passage of time and the fleeting nature of youth.

Peter Nero is still alive.

Further Listening:

Young, Warm, And Wonderful (RCA LSP-2484) 1962
Hail The Conquering Nero (RCA LSP-2638) 1963

Songs You Won't Forget (RCA LSP-2935) 1964
The Screen Scene (RCA LSP-3496) 1966
Plays 'Born Free' (RCA Camden CAS-2139) 1967
Plays 'Love Is Blue' and Ten Other Great Songs (RCA LSP-3936) 1968
Love Trip (RCA LSP-4205) 1968
I've Gotta Be Me (Columbia CS 9800) 1969
From "Hair" To Hollywood (Columbia CS 9907) 1970
Summer Of '42 (Columbia C 31105) 1972
The First Time Ever I Saw Your Face (Columbia KC-31335) 1972
The World Of Peter Nero (Columbia KG-31982) [2] 1973

Russ Conway

Key Recording: The New Side Of Russ Conway

Released as a Vinyl LP
Tracklist:
A-Side: 'Aquarius'/'Little Green Apples'/'My Way'/'Up Up And Away'/'Gwyneth Gwen'/'Aranjuez Mon Amour'
B-Side: 'Something'/'Hava Nagila'/'Greensleeves'/'The Fool On The Hill'/'Bells Away'/'The Valley Of The Shadow Of Tears'
Label: Columbia Records
Release date: 1971

Russ Conway was born Trevor Herbert Stanford on 2 September 1925 in Bristol, England, the youngest of three brothers. His father was a commercial salesman. His mother, a housewife who played piano. Having won a scholarship to Bristol Cathedral Choir, he left school at fourteen but ended up in Borstal for three years for stealing from his employer, a solicitor. However, it was during those four years of incarceration that he honed his juvenile piano-playing skills. He served in the Royal Navy during WW2, winning a Distinguished Service Medal for 'gallantry and devotion to duty' while stationed on a minesweeper. He famously lost the tip of a finger while using a bread slicer. Choosing not to be demobbed after the war, he was nevertheless discharged from the Navy in 1948 on grounds of ill health. He then joined the Merchant Navy, serving as a steward with P&O, but ill health again forced him to leave.

Conway, who never learnt to read music, began playing the piano in London clubs and soon won a record deal with EMI, who saw him as their answer to Decca's Winifred Atwell. A&R man Norman Newell saw him fitting in well to a growing adult-orientated album market, where the older generation were uninterested in the new skiffle and rock 'n' roll music of the young. Newell suggested he change his name to Ross Conway and he never looked back. Before releasing his first record, an EP in 1957 on Columbia Records, *Party Pops* (SEG 7847), he worked with England singer, Joan Regan, and English superstar of stage and screen, Gracie Fields.

Proving to be a brilliantly gifted accompanist, he was much in demand with the big bands and orchestras of the day, performing with the likes of the hugely popular Ted Heath Band, which featured singing stars such as Lita Roza and Dickie Valentine. Consequently, it wasn't long before he was topping the bill in his own right, becoming renowned for his trademark 'twinkling' smile.

Pianists were always very popular in the UK, particularly in pubs, where a piano can provide a kind of music-hall melodiousness in which everyone can tap their feet, raise their glasses and sing along. Conway's toe-tapping, honk-tonk style scored a number of big hits in the UK, most notably a number one with 'Side Saddle' (Columbia DB 4256,1959), a number five with 'China Tea'(Columbia DB 4337, 1959) and another number one with 'Roulette'(Columbia DB 4298, 1959). In the US, he had minor hits in 1959 on Capital and Cub Records with the same singles, but scored bigger hits in 1958 with 'Got A Match' (number 21), in 1960 with 'Fings Ain't Wot They Used T'be' (number 12) and 1962 with 'Always You and Me' (number 19).

Conway could, however, also play identifiably easy listening tunes, complete with lush strings and 'wordless' singers, most notably when playing with the Geoff Love, Tony Osborne, Phillip Green and Michael Collins Orchestras, with the chorus provided by either The Williams Singers or The Mike Sammes Singers. His performances included such easy listening classics as 'Theme From A Summer Place', 'Passing Breeze', 'Always', 'The Warsaw Concerto', 'Ebbtide' and many other easy listening classics. He released a Liberace-inspired album in 1960 that was orientated more to light classical music than easy listening. It reached number five on the UK album chart. His first album of definably easy listening arrangements, *The New Side Of Russ Conway* (CMS 1005), seen above, was an album of new and old pop standards. While his toe-tapping hits remained ever-popular, his easy listening albums contained no hint of his honky-tonk style and were hugely popular, along with his personal appearances at venues like The London Palladium, on TV and radio. His easy listening style could reflect the more up-tempo sound of the beat era's pop hits. It was as far away from Muzak as one could get, but still retained that air of romanticism, particularly with tracks like 'Aranjuez Mon Amour' and 'Love Is All', that is at the heart of easy listening music and which adult audiences delighted in. He was one of Britain's biggest-selling recording artists before the Beat era, selling more than 30 million records. In 1957, while sheet music was still selling well, he topped the chart for a total of six months with three compositions under his real name of Trevor Standford.

As has already been alluded to, Conway was dogged with ill health, which forced him to take breaks from performing. He drank heavily, smoked as many as 80 cigarettes a day and became addicted to anti-depressants. He suffered a stroke and developed stomach cancer, from both of which he, however, recovered to remain active on stage and on

TV. In 1994, he starred in a French and Saunders' 1994 Christmas special, playing his 1959 evergreen hit, 'Side Saddle'. In the same year, he made a cameo appearance in their TV spoof of the film *The Piano*. He gave his last performance in 2000 when he hosted a show to celebrate his 75th birthday, which included many of his old surviving showbiz pals, not least of all Joan Regan.

'Up Up And Away'

'Up Up And Away' showcases his virtuoso piano playing with dazzling flair. His nimble fingers dance across the keys, weaving a tapestry of melodic and harmonic brilliance. The piano becomes an extension of his musical soul, as he effortlessly navigates intricate runs and cascading arpeggios. Each note is delivered with precision, resonating with a lively energy that lifts the spirits of listeners. Conway's performance exudes an infectious sense of joy and an undeniable mastery of his instrument, making his rendition of 'Up Up And Away' a worthy addition to easy listening piano-driven arrangements.

'Greensleeves'

Russ Conway's rendition of 'Greensleeves' marks a delightful shift from his pub-style piano playing to a more inviting and upbeat easy listening genre. This enchanting musical journey unfolds with a drum fill, leading to a ragtime-style piano accompaniment. This is supported by a guitar playing a syncopated chord structure, with an infusion of a short but decisive decrescendo from a Hammond organ. It ends as it started with a Buddy Rich-style closing drum fill. It is the timeless courtly melody of 'Greensleeves' that stops the whole thing from getting out of control, happily leaving us with what can only be described as another of Conway's quintessential easy listening arrangements, which my musical mentor Darren Nicholas describes as a masterpiece.

Russ Conway died on 16 November 2000 in Eastbourne, East Sussex, England.

Further Listening:

The New Side Of Russ Conway (CMS 1005) 1971
Side Saddle (Delta CD 6455) 2012
Party Pops (Columbia 33 HP 157) 1961

Winifred Atwell

Key Recording: 'The Streets Of Sorrento' b/w 'The Hope Waltz' (Featuring Cyril Stapleton And His Orchestra)

Released as a 7" 45-rpm Single
Label: Decca
Release date: August 1957

Key Recording: The Plush Piano Of...

Released as a Vinyl LP

Tracklist:

A-Side: 'As Long As He Needs Me' (Lionel Bart)/'Misty' (Erroll Garner)/'Go Away, Little Girl' (Carole King, Gerry Goffin)/'Portrait Of My Love' (Carole King)/'I Only Have Eyes For You' (Cyril Ornadel)/'Birth Of The Blues' (David West, Lew Brown)

B-Side: 'Exodus' (Ernest Gold)/'Theme From Monte Carlo' (Robert Mellin)/'I Believe' (Buddy DeSylva)/'What Kind Of Fool Am I' (Anthony Newley, Leslie Bricusse)/'Smile' (Charlie Chaplin)/'Cuando Calienta El Aol' (Carlos Alberto Martinoli, Carlos Riguel, Mario Rigual)

Label: Blue Pie Records

Release date: 1960

Una Winifred Atwell was born in Tunapuna, Trinidad and Tobago, on 27 February (or 27 April) 1910 (or 1914). She was another hugely popular pianist in Britain and Australia. She and her parents lived in Jubilee Street. She played the piano from a young age and achieved considerable local popularity. She played for American servicemen at the island's US Air Force base and it was they who told her she should try playing boogie-woogie style. She took to it immediately and although she trained to be a pharmacist and was expected to join the family pharmacy business, she decided on a showbiz career.

Atwell left Trinidad in the early 1940s and travelled to the United States to study with Alexander Borovsky. Finding the prevailing racial discrimination stymying her chances of career advancement, she left in 1945 for England and was soon to be heard playing on BBC light music radio shows. She studied at the Royal Academy of Music, where she became the first female pianist to achieve top grades. To support her studies, she played rags at London clubs and theatres, where she was discovered by Bernard Delfont. Under his guidance, her career blossomed and she secured a record contract with Decca London and was soon enjoying Top Ten hit records on the US and UK music charts with tunes like 'Black and White Rag' (Decca F 9790), 1951), 'Coronation Rag' (London 1343, 1953) and 'The Left Bank' (London 1680, 1956). She was the first black artist to sell a million records and is the only artist ever to be awarded two silver and gold discs for record sales of piano music. Following in the footsteps of Mantovani and Eddie Calvert, she had only the third-ever instrumental number one with 'Let's Have Another Party', which topped the charts for five weeks in December 1954, also making her the first black artist to have a number one hit record in the UK. As well as record sales, she sold millions of copies of sheet music.

Her easy listening credentials might be questioned as her playing style was mainly boogie-woogie and ragtime, but she did release equally popular easy listening albums, complete with voiceless choir, with songs like 'As Long As He Needs Me', 'C'est L'amour', 'Greensleeves', 'Bewitched, Bothered and Bewildered', 'Soft Summer Breeze', 'Smile' and so on. She did have one US hit with 'Moonlight Gambler' (original release cat. number not found, but available on *Black And White Rag* (Jasmine JASCD756)), which went to number 16 on the *Billboard* chart. While being slightly jaunty, it can only be described as easy listening, with its wordless choir sounding as hauntingly otherworldly as the song's title might suggest.

After a hugely successful tour of Australia, she decided to make her home there, while continuing to perform sell-out concerts worldwide.

'The Streets Of Sorrento'

The piece opens with a lively and infectious melody that immediately captures the listener's attention. Atwell's piano technique is characterised by energetic stride piano playing, combining rapid, rhythmic patterns and percussive chords. This dynamic approach creates a sense of exuberance and joy, making 'The Streets Of Sorrento' an enjoyable and engaging piece. Strings fill the musical landscape, providing a lush backdrop for the evolving melody.

The title evokes a sense of Italian charm and a picturesque seaside town, and Atwell's music mirrors this imagery. As the composition progresses, it takes on a playful and lively character, inviting the listener to imagine a bustling, cheerful atmosphere. Atwell's performance not only showcases her technical prowess but also her ability to infuse the music with personality and a sense of storytelling.

Winifred Atwell died on 28 February 1983 in Sydney, Australia.

Further Listening:

Double 7 (Decca DFE6405) 1961
Queen Of Honky Tonk (SCLA 1222) 1967
Black And White Magic (London Records LB 732) 1956
Around The World In 80 Tunes (Decca SKL4012) 1958

Ferrante And Teicher

Key Recording: The World's Greatest Themes

Released as a Vinyl LP

Tracklist:

A-Side: 'Theme From 'The Apartment'' (Charles Williams)/'Love Affair (Rachmaninoff's 2nd Piano Concerto – 3rd Movement)'/'Fantasy d'amour (Chopin's 'Fantaisie impromptu')'/'Dreams (Schumann's Träumerei)'/'Lonesome Heart (Tchaikovsky's 'None But The Lonely Heart')'/'Lonely Room (Adolph Deutsch)'

B-Side: 'Lovers In Paradise (Borodin's 'Polovetsian Dances')'/'Dream Rhapsody (Rachmaninoff's 2nd Piano Concerto – 1st and 2nd Movements)'/'Romance (Rubinstein's 'Melody Of Dreams')'/'Forever Loved (Tchaikovsky's 5th Symphony)'/'Lover's Lament (Beethoven's 'Moonlight Sonata')'/'Lovers By

Starlight (Beethoven)'
Label: United Artists
Release date: 1960

Arthur Ferrante was born in New York City, US, on 7 September 1921. Louis Teicher was born in Wilkes-Barre, Pennsylvania, on 24 August 1924. Playing not one but two pianos were the duo, Ferrante and Teicher. First meeting as children when pupils at Juilliard School, Manhattan, they displayed remarkable musical talents from a very early age and began performing as a piano duo while still in school. In 1947, they launched a full-time concert career, at first playing nightclubs, then quickly moving up to playing classical music with orchestral backing. It was obvious they were searching for new sounds and they experimented with avant-garde arrangements. Stuffing their pianos with paper, sticks, rubber, wood blocks, metal bars, chains, glass, mallets, and so on, they were able to produce a variety of bizarre sounds that sometimes resembled percussion instruments and at other times resulted in special effects that sounded as if they were electronically synthesised. They released two albums incorporating all these weird and other-worldly sounds, *Blast Off!* (ABCS-285, 1959) and *Heavenly Sounds In Hi-Fi* (ABCS 221, 1957). Depending on one's musical tastes, the music was either extraordinary but fascinating, or it was just plain best avoided in favour of something more accessible.

Their recording and concert work was good as far as it went, but it was not making them a living. Then in 1960, they met renowned Muzak arranger Nick Perito, at United Artists. Here was a man who knew how to make a commercial success out of music, be it in films or on records. For 40 years, he was Perry Como's closest musical collaborator, helping him to make numerous hit singles and albums. He got Ferrante and Teicher to add orchestral and choral backing to their playing and, by doing so, turned them into the highly paid performers they very quickly became. It was a short leap to easy listening arrangements. They said they never regretted 'deserting' the classics: it brought them to the attention of a much bigger audience, which meant '…we no longer have to teach to make a living'.

Their first album, *The World's Greatest Themes*, produced by Don Costa, with orchestra conducted by Nick Perito, though, in fact, did feature in the main much loved classical music themes. The arrangements all incorporated the innovations and hallmarks of the top-selling easy listening band leaders of the time: Paul Weston's and Jackie Gleason's unabashed romanticism, Mantovani's and Percy Faith's lush strings and Ray Conniff's wordless chorus. Most of the albums that followed focussed on, as was normal and indeed expected now in easy listening albums, pop standards and hits, as well as songs from what would later be called the 'American Songbook'.

The first track on *The World's Greatest Themes* was 'Theme From 'The Apartment'' (UA 231, 1960), originally composed by Charles Williams for the 1949 British film *The Romantic Age*. The tune was first recorded in

1949 by the Charles Williams Concert Orchestra and was entitled 'Jealous Lover' (Columbia D.X. 1569, 12" Shellac 78 RPM). Ferrante and Teicher's arrangement could not have been more easy listening if it had tried – from the very first note, there were swirling strings and a celestial wordless chorus – and was a Top Ten hit for the piano-playing duo in 1960. They had other Top Ten hits with 'Theme From Exodus' (UA 274, 1960), 'Tonight' (UA 373, 1961) and 'Midnight Cowboy' (UA 50554, 1969).

As much as their best-selling albums, what also marked them out was their live concert performances with pop orchestras. They thrilled their audiences with irresistible, sparklingly inventive performances, which they preferred to call their 'two-man show(s)'. Their 1970 hit single rendition of Bob Dylan's 'Lay Lady Lay' (UA 59646, 1970) clearly demonstrates how they liked to 'mix-it-up' with inventive piano and orchestra instrumentation by adding a reverberated guitar and brass. Such playfulness in their music made their 'two-man shows' hugely popular, helping them to sell millions of albums.

'Theme From 'The Apartment"

This track is a compelling example that highlights the mesmerising capabilities of double pianos. It is best heard through headphones.

The piece begins with a lush and emotive melody, with the pianos creating a rich and full sound. The two pianos complement each other, creating a harmonious blend of tones that adds depth and complexity to the music. They are supported by the richly layered sounds of strings.

The interplay between the pianos is a central feature of the piece. Ferrante and Teicher skillfully trade off one another, showcasing their exceptional synchronisation and artistic chemistry. The composition's structure, with one piano often taking the lead while the other provides an intricate accompaniment, adds an intriguing layer of musical conversation. The music possesses a romantic and cinematic quality, evoking a sense of intimacy and nostalgia that aligns with the concept of an apartment setting.

Overall, it is a captivating example of how double pianos can elevate a musical composition, offering a unique and engaging listening experience. The piece not only showcases the technical prowess of the pianists but also their ability to create a lush and emotive musical tapestry that resonates with audiences, making it a cherished gem in the world of piano duets.

Louis Teicher died on 3 August 2008 in Highlands, North Carolina, US. Arthur Ferrante died of natural causes on 19 September 2009 in Longboat Key, Florida, US.

Further Listening:

The World's Greatest Themes (UAS-6121) 1960
West Side Story And Other Motion Picture And Broadway Hits (UAS-6166) 1961
Love Themes (WWS-8514) 1962

Tonight (UAS-6171) 1962
The Keys To Her Apartment (UAS-6247) 1962
Love Themes From Cleopatra (UAS-6290) 1963
The People's Choice (UAS-6385) 1964
By Popular Demand (UAS-6416) 1965
You Asked For It! (UAS-3526) 1966
'A Man And A Woman' And Other Motion Picture Themes (UAS-6572) 1967
Live For Life And Other Great Themes (UAS-6632) 1967
The Painted Desert (UAS-6636) 1968
A Bouquet Of Hits (UAS-6659) 1968
Love In The Generation Gap (UAS-6671) 1968
Midnight Cowboy (UAS-6725) 1969
Getting Together (UAS-5501) 1970
It's Too Late (UAS-5531) 1971
Play The Hit Themes (UAS-5588) 1972
Hear And Now (UA-LA018F) 1973
Dial "M" For Music (UA-LA195F) 1974
Beautiful...Beautiful (UA-LA316-G) 1975
The Carpenters' Songbook (UA-LA490G) 1976
Piano Portraits (UA-LA-585-G) 1976
Feelings (UA-LA662G) 1977
You Light Up My Life (UA-LA908G) 1978
All Time Great Movie Themes (CD EMI E2-0777-7-98823-2-8) 1993
Instrumental Favorites (CD Time Life Music S21-18343 R986-08) 1995
Great 1970s Motion Picture Themes (CD Capitol 30518) 2001

Ronnie Aldrich

Key Recording: Melody And Percussion For Two Pianos

Released as a Vinyl LP
Tracklist:
A-side: 'Unforgettable' (Gordon)/'Secret Love' (Webster, Fain)/'To Each His Own' (Livingston, Evans)/'Ruby' (Roemheld, Parish)/'April In Portugal' (Larue, Kennedy, Ferrao)/'My One And Only Love' (Wood, Mellin)
B-side: 'Autumn Leaves' (Prevert, Mercer, Kosma)/'Misty' (Garner Burke)/'Golden Earrings' (Livingston, Evans)/'Young At Heart' (Leigh, Richards)/'April Fool' (Webster, Fain)/'The Gypsy' (Reid, Lanjean)
Label: London
Release date: 1962

Ronnie Aldrich was born in Erith, Kent, UK, on 15 February 1916. He was educated at The Harvey Grammar School, Folkestone, Kent, UK and taught violin at the Guildhall School of Music and Drama in London. In the 1930s, he was in India playing jazz, while in the 1940s, he was in The Squadronaires.

He led the band from 1951 when it was billed as 'Ronnie Aldrich and The Squadronaires'. It disbanded in 1951.

In 1961, UK Decca Records invented what was called 'Phase 4 Stereo'. This allowed music to be recorded and played back on two channels, extreme right and extreme left. It was this innovation that allowed Aldrich to record his complex piano arrangements, often sounding as if he was playing not one, but two pianos. The wizardry of Decca's sound engineers – under the expert guidance of several producers, including Hugh Mendl, Mark White, Tony D'Amato, and particularly Arthur Bannister, who knew how to balance the Aldrich pianos – working closely with Aldrich himself, meant they were able to control the volume of his piano playing in the stereo channels to give the two-piano effect.

As was usual in easy listening by now, Aldrich would choose a pop song and then start picking out the melody in single notes, before adding his carefully crafted lush string arrangements, often adding percussion. He usually worked with the London Festival Orchestra.

Aldrich produced 19 wonderful easy listening albums for Decca's Phase 4 Stereo Series. He was often referred to as 'England's Ferrante and Teicher', who, it will be remembered, did, in fact, play two pianos. He went on to make numerous other easy listening albums and was appointed musical director at Thames Television, where he provided the zany music for comedian Benny Hill's slap-stick comedy series, *The Benny Hill Show*.

'Unforgettable'

'Unforgettable' is a notable arrangement that exemplifies the innovative stereo recording techniques employed during the Phase 4 Stereo era at Decca Records. This rendition stands out for its ability to create the illusion of two pianos played by a single pianist.

Decca's recording engineers, directed by Aldrich, were keen on experimenting with stereo sound to enhance the listening experience. In 'Unforgettable', Ronnie Aldrich's piano performance is recorded in a manner that gives the impression of two separate pianos, positioned in the left and right audio channels. This stereo separation cleverly emphasises a piano's full range and depth. Similarly, Aldrich uses the same technique to deliver a listening experience with percussion, using bongos and chimes. Later in the piece, he again uses the technology to create a call-and-response between a xylophone and a jazz guitar.

Aldrich's precise use of dynamics and stereo panning techniques allows the listener to hear a spatial divide between each of the key instruments within the piece. The interplay between the left and right channels further amplifies the musicality, creating a rich and immersive auditory experience. 'Unforgettable' indeed. Again, it is best heard through headphones.

Ronnie Aldrich died on 30 September 1993 on the Isle of Man, UK.

Further Listening:

The albums below are mostly part of Decca/London's Phase 4 Stereo series.
Melody And Percussion For Two Pianos (SP-44007) 1962
The Magnificent Pianos Of Ronnie Aldrich (sp-44029) 1963
The Romantic Pianos Of Ronnie Aldrich (SP-44042) 1964
Magic Moods Of Ronnie Aldrich (SP-44062) 1965
That Aldrich Feeling (SP-44070) 1965
Two Pianos In Hollywood (SP-44092) 1967
Two Pianos Today! (SP-44100) 1967
This Way "In" (SP-44116) 1968
For Young Lovers (SP-44108) 1968
Destination Love (SP-44135) 1969
It's Happening Now (SP-44127) 1969
Here Come The Hits! (SP-44143) 1970
Close To You (sp-44156) 1970
Love Story (SP-44162) 1971
Come To Where The Love Is (SP-44190) 1972
Invitation To Love (SP-44176) 1972
In The Gentle Hours (SP-44221) 1975
Love (SP-44253) 1975
Reflections (SP-44264) 1976
Webb Country (SP-44278) 1977
Evergreen (SP-44286) 1977
Emotions (SP-44310) 1978
One Fine Day (Amberjack AJK-902) 1981
Imagine (Audio Fidelity AFE-1026) 1981
Beautiful Music (Audio Fidelity AFE-6306) 1982
Music For All Seasons (CD Realm 1CD-8204) 1992
Twin Piano Magic (CD Rebound Records 314-520-234-2) 1994

Bert Kaempfert

Key Recording: Wonderland By Night

Released as a Vinyl lP
Tracklist:
A-Side: 'Wonderland By Night (Wunderland Bei Nacht)' (Klaus Gunter-Neumann)/'Vie En Rose' (Edith Piaf, Louiguy)/'Happiness Never Comes Too Late (Das Glück Kommt Nie Zu Spät)' (Bert Kaempfert)/'On The Alamo' (Gus Kahn, Isham Jones)/'As I Love You' (Jay Livingston,Ray Evans)/'Dreaming The Blues' (Bert Kaempfert)
B-Side: 'Tammy' (Jay Livingston, Ray Evans)/'The Aim Of My Desires (Das Ziel Meiner Wünsche)' (Peter Moesser)/'This Song Is Yours Alone (Dieses Lied Gehört Nur Dir)' (Bert Kaempfert)/'Drifting And Dreaming (Sweet Paradise)' (Van Alstyne, Schmidt, Gillespie, Curtin)/'Stay With Me' (Bert Kaempfert)/'Lullaby For Lovers' (Bert Kaempfert)

Label: Decca
Release date: 1960

Bert Kaempfert was born in Hamburg, Germany, on 16 October 1923. A child prodigy, he studied at the Hamburg School of Music. Joining Hans Busch's popular Radio Danzig band, Kaempfert, a multi-instrumentalist, created a peculiarly German kind of swing music, arranging it to suit the strict tempo style of German war-time dance. The tune that he gave back to America was, however, a beautiful piece of easy listening music called 'Wonderland By Night'. Despite having become an arranger and A&R man for Polydor Records, he could not get it released in Germany, so he took it to Decca in New York. They released it in the autumn of 1960 and it instantly became a worldwide smash, shooting straight to the top of *Billboard*'s Hot 100 chart and becoming a million seller. Kaempfert had added something new: a haunting solo trumpet, played by Charles Tabor, and muted brass. Although Percy Faith used strings to bring out the melody, you would still consider strings in the main to be used as an accompaniment to fill space. The move by Kaempfert to the use of a brass instrument, e.g. the trumpet, as the solo lead, pushes the melody even further to the fore. The trumpet is played like a lead vocal around which the musical 'background' acts like a stage setting. The muted brass is utilised to create contrast, effectively replacing the lush strings, but still giving the piece its uplifting, dreamy mood, so much now the trademark of what was becoming 'easy listening' music. Helping to achieve the latter is a choir, the male voices humming the melody on top of the musted brass, while the female vocals soar angelically.

Kaempfert followed 'Wonderland By Night' with the top-selling album *That Happy Feeling*, which was later released worldwide as *A Swinging Safari*. The eponymous tune, 'A Swinging Safari', continued to take easy listening in a new direction. Its distinctively catchy main theme is played on a piccolo. A trumpet solo is played by Manfred 'Fred' Moch. And there are again the soaring 'wordless' female vocals. While Bert Kampfert's single, 'A Swing Safari', itself failed to chart, a cover by Billy Vaughan, with an almost identical arrangement, was a number 10 hit in the *Billboard* charts.

Bert Kaempfert went on to compose some easy listening classics, notably, 'Strangers In The Night', and a tune called 'Moon Over Naples' that, when lyrics were added, became 'Spanish Eyes', both becoming easy listening classics. Of course, 'Stranger In The Night', with added English lyrics by Charles Singleton and Eddie Snyder, was a huge hit for Frank Sinatra in 1969, while 'Spanish Eyes' was a million seller for Al Martino in 1966. He also wrote 'Wooden Heart' sung by Elvis Presley in the film *G.I. Blues*.

'Wonderland By Night'

It begins with a grand entrance by Kaempfert's trumpet, accompanied by a vocal exclamation from a male chorus line. This introductory flourish transitions smoothly into a swinging double bass, providing percussive support, and a clean jazz guitar offering a solo with lower-toned, almost bass-like qualities. The single trumpet takes the lead in carrying the melody.

The piece is primarily driven by a choral arrangement, with the main vocal delivery coming from a female chorus, accompanied by occasional male vocals in the background. The trombone and woodwind instruments provide additional support. This pattern continues for the majority of the song, with Kaempfert's often muted trumpet weaving in and out, enhancing both the verses and choruses.

The song consistently maintains a prominent jazz ambience, ending as it began, with a trumpet solo that neatly brings it to a fitting conclusion.

'Swinging Safari'

The track commences with Bert Kaempfert's distinctive percussive style, featuring a brushed snare drum. This is swiftly followed by a swinging rhythm, accompanied by piccolos, which introduces the instantly recognisable hook that has endeared this song to many. Prior to the entry of the trumpets, there is a noteworthy presence of an acoustic guitar, reminiscent of a ska influence, propelling the rhythm section. This is complemented by a muted jazz guitar, executing a clean walking bass line that employs a combination of scale tones and chromatic runs to outline the underlying chord progression.

Throughout the song, the core elements consist of percussion, acoustic guitar and jazz guitar, briefly receding to make way for a vocal choral interlude. This break in the instrumentation adds a touch of variety. Midway through the composition, the main hook resurfaces, played once again by the piccolos, disrupting the established structure. Nevertheless, it is predominantly the rhythm section that propels the song along, with the trumpets taking the lead in delivering the main melody. This musical arrangement is occasionally enriched by the subtle addition of strings, which provide additional layers and nuances to the overall composition, contributing to its dynamic range and texture.

Bert Kaempfert died on 21 June 1980.

Further Listening:

Wonderland By Night (Decca DL-74101) 1960
The Wonderland Of Bert Kaempfert (Decca DL-74117) 1961
Afrikaan Beat (Decca DL-74273) 1962
That Happy Feeling (Decca DL-74305) 1962
Living It Up! (Decca DL-74374) 1963
Lights Out, Sweet Dreams (Decca DL-74265) 1963
Blue Midnight (Decca DL-74569) 1965
That Latin Feeling (Decca DL-74490) 1964
The Magic Music Of Faraway Places (Decca DL-74616) 1965

Bye Bye Blues (Decca DL-74693) 1966
Strangers In The Night (Decca DL-74795) 1966
Hold Me (Decca DL-74860) 1967
The World We Knew (Decca DL-74925) 1967
...Love That (Decca DL-74986) 1968
My Way Of Life (Decca DL-75059) 1968
Warm And Wonderful (Decca DL-75089) 1969
Traces Of Love (Decca DL-75140) 1969
The Kaempfert Touch (Decca DL-75175) 1970
Orange Colored Sky (Decca DL-75256) 1971
Bert Kaempfert Now! (Decca DL-75305) 1971
Fabulous Fifties...And New Delights (MCA-314) 1973
Strangers In The Night (Longines Symphonette Box Set) (LWS-299) [5]
Instrumental Favorites (CD Time Life Music R986-18) 1996
The Very Best Of Bert Kaempfert (CD Taragon 1014) 1996

James Last

Key Recording: Non-Stop Dancing 1965 (28 Hits Für Ihre Part)

Released as a Vinyl LP
Tracklist:
A-side:
Rock Fox (3:22): 'Don't Ha, Ha' (Smith, Vincent, R. M. Siegel)/'Shake Hands' (Gaze, Relin)/'Can't Buy Me Love' (Lennon, McCartney)
Slop (4:25): 'Skinny Minnie' (Keefer, Haley, Dafra, Montague, Lilibert, Gabler)/'Do Wah Diddy, Diddy' (Greenwich, Barry, Simson)/'Clap Hands' (H. Last)
Slow Beat (3:21): 'Pretty Woman' (Lilibert, Roy Orbison, Bill Dees)/'Das Ist Die Frage Aller Fragen' (Blecher, Leiber, Spector)
Shake (3:58): 'Eight Days A Week' (Lennon, McCartney)/'Kiddy, Kiddy, Kiss Me' (Munro)/'Good Bye, Good Bye, Good Bye' (Bradtke, Mayer)
Blue Beat (3:12): 'My Boy Lollipop' (Robert, Hertha, Spencer)/'Zwei Mädchen Aus Germany' (Buchholz, Loose)/'Tennessee Waltz' (King, Stewart, Hansen)
B-side:
Skiffle Beat (3:22): 'Memphis Tennessee' (Berry, Montague, Lilibert)/'A Hard Day's Night' (Lennon, McCartney)/'I Feel Fine' (Lennon, McCartney)
Shake (5:07): 'No Reply' (Lennon, McCartney)/'Kiss And Shake' (Loose, W. Last)/'Downtown' (Blecher, Hatch)
Slop Beguine (4:27): 'Cinderella Baby' (Bruhn, Loose)/'Wer Kann Das Schon?' (Stahl, Weigend)/'Das War Mein Schönster Tanz' (Smith, Hertha)
Slow Beat (3:26): 'Rag Doll' (Crewe, Gaudio, Bader)/'Melancholie' (Fuchsberger)
Shake Twist (4:40): 'I Want To Hold Your Hand' (Lennon, McCartney)/'Sie Liebt Dich' (Lennon, McCartney)/'I Should Have Known Better' (Lennon, McCartney)
Label: Polydor Records
Release date: 1965

Hans Last was born on 17 April 1929 in Bremen, Germany. WWII shaped his early life and start in music. He was studying music in school, but Bremen was heavily bombed by the Allies and his school was closed down. The only route open to him then was to enrol as a cadet at the military music school in Frankfurt, where he studied brass instruments and piano. In 1945, its buildings were destroyed by allied bombing and in the chaos that ensued, the school as such simply ceased to exist and the students were evacuated to Buckenburg, near Hanover, to continue their training.

Luckily for Last, when the war ended, he found himself in the American occupation zone. He was recruited by Hans-Gunter Oesterreich, who organised entertainment for the American troops to play the piano and eventually double bass in clubs and bars. It was his start as a professional musician. In the same year, he joined the dance orchestra of Radio Bremen, playing bass. Last had two brothers who were also keen musicians and with them as band members, in 1948, he formed a small jazz band with Karl-Heinz Becker. It consisted of 13 musicians and was called the Last-Becker Ensemble. In 1950, and for the next two years, Last was voted Best Bass Musician Of The Year by popular men's magazine *Die Gondel*. The band played in Frankfurt's first jazz festival. Following his successes, Last was asked by Radio Bremen to form a string orchestra, which was to give live concerts twice a week. He began to gain a reputation as an arranger of talent but felt Radio Bremen was limiting his chances of reaching a wider audience. He moved to Hamburg and joined the dance orchestra of broadcaster Nordwestdeutscher Rundfunk (NDR). As well as playing acoustic and, latterly, electric bass in the orchestra, he was an arranger, often for famous names making appearances with the orchestra. He toured Europe with pop singer Helmut Zacharias as his musical director. He was asked in 1955 by composer Michael Jary, to write the music for the musical comedy film, *Wie Werde Ich Filmstar?*.

Becoming a much sought-after arranger, he was signed by Polydor Records in 1964, though not to make his own records just yet. Like so many of the great band leaders before and after, he had an idea in his head of the kind of music he wanted to make. He released a few albums of re-arranged 1940s and 1950s pop standards, plus a conventional, if more popularly arranged, album of classical music. They didn't sell well. Hans Last was not happy. He liked to party and he loved pop music and thought that an album of non-stop hits played in the background would give a great atmosphere to parties at home. He later said that:

> as a young boy, I listened with my father to a radio program with a Danish channel, where they were broadcasting with a live audience and you heard music through the clattering of glasses and bags. Even as a child, I experienced the special atmosphere in the broadcast. The memory of these radio broadcasts is actually the basis of my party sound.

The new Liverpool sound of the Beatles was sweeping the world and Last added that he asked himself, 'why not make the music of young people danceable for the older generations?' The fact that his emphasis was on the older generation was the point. He was, in effect, re-inventing easy listening music for the adult world of a new era. To their ears, 60s pop music was just a racket; Hans Last, or James Last, as he was now to be known – his Polydor Records believing it would have more universal appeal – would bring out of the beat-dominated racket what could be its rhythms and melodies. His first album *Non-Stop Dancing '65*, released in that year, was a huge success. 'Happy music' had been invented and it became James Last's trademark sound. In terms of qualifying as easy listening music, perhaps this is all one needs to know. In a world that is always fraught with anxiety of some sort or other, his music, to quote again the Anglo-Saxon poem, 'Solomon and Saturn', '...relieve(d) the heart's mood of every man... heal(ed) the distress of daily living...'. And this was the job of all easy listening music, not least of all in terms of how it was marketed by its record companies, and they, of course, knew their marketing demographic well.

His albums were orchestrated collections of non-stop hit records segueing into one another, with a gently driving bass beat (remember he was an award-winning bass player in Germany long before he groped his way into easy listening success at Polydor Records), irresistibly backed by Ray Conniff's invention of the 'wordless' choir. Last's choir, however, was not 'instrumentalised' in the way Ray Conniff's was, but rather, they gave a listener the sense that it was the sound of people at a gathering partying and singing along to the latest hits.

Last also occasionally recorded albums of conventional easy listening music and 'updated' classical music and Christmas tunes.

He became the golden era's biggest star, certainly in terms of record sales and live audience attendance. He went on to record 30 million-selling 'Non-Stop' dance albums, plus numerous variations of the theme with album titles such as *Beach Party*, *Sax A Go-Go*, *Trumper A Go-Go*, *Humba A Go-Go* and many more. His name was known to music lovers across all pop genres and lovers of popularly accessible classical music arrangements. He either made you put your fingers down your throat, or he filled you with varying degrees of pure delight; he might even have made you want to give expression to that sense of euphoria by getting up and taking your loved one in your arms and, well, looking her or him in the eye and seeing in them a reflection that told you, yes, they loved you and all was right with the world.

He toured the world giving live performances of irresistibly 'happy music'. As a result, his record sales topped well over 200 million worldwide, winning him 200 gold and 14 platinum discs. This was despite his music being dismissed by his critics as 'acoustic porridge' and he himself as 'the king of elevator music'.

'Rock Fox'

'Rock Fox' is a medley of 'Don't Ha Ha', 'Shake Hands' and 'Can't Buy Me Love'. It is an electrifying party piece that infuses the exuberance of rock music with added vocals, creating a dynamic and unforgettable musical experience.

The song bursts to life with a vigorous rock rhythm, driven by a pulsating beat, spirited electric guitars and a propulsive bassline. It serves as a sonic invitation to the dance floor, encouraging everyone to join in the festivities. As the music gains momentum, the vocals make their entrance, adding an exciting layer to the composition. The lyrics are often spirited and celebratory, enhancing the party atmosphere.

Throughout 'Rock Fox', the vocals and instrumentals collaborate seamlessly, creating a harmonious fusion of rock elements and catchy melodies. The dynamic interplay between the lead vocalist and the instrumentation keeps the energy levels high and the audience engaged.

As the song progresses, it builds to euphoric crescendos, encouraging enthusiastic sing-alongs and lively dancing. Its spirited and infectious nature makes it an ideal party piece, setting the stage for a memorable and joyous celebration. James Last's arrangement and the added vocals ensure that the party is in full swing, making it an essential track for any festive gathering.

James Last died on 9 June 2015 in Palm Beach, Florida, US.

Further Listening:

Hammond À Gogo (Polydor 249043) 1965
Non Stop Dancing '66 (Polydor LPHM46995) 1965
Beat In Sweet (Polydor 249002) 1965
Instrumentals Forever (Polydor 184 059) 1966
Christmas Dancing (Polydor 543010) 1966
That's Life (Polydor 184 092) 1967
Games That Lovers Play (Polydor 184093) 1967
Humba Humba À Gogo (Polydor 249205) 1968
Trumpet À Gogo 3 (Polydor 2489506) 1968
Beachparty (Polydor 2371188) 1970
Happyning (Polydor 2371 133) 1971
In Concert (Polydor 2371191) 1971
Voodoo Party (Polydor 2371 235) 1971
Love Must Be The Reason (Polydor 2371 281) 1972
Non Stop Dancing 1973 (Polydor 2371 376) 1972
Violins in Love (Polydor 2371 520) 1974
In The Mood for Trumpets (Polydor 2371 548) 1975
Rock Me Gently (Polydor 2371 584) 1975
Non Stop Dancing 1977 (Polydor 249 384) 1976
Copacabana – Dancing (Polydor 2371 929) 1979

Paul Mauriat

Key Recording: 'Love Is Blue'

Released as a 7" 45-rpm Single
Label: Phillips
Release date: 1967

Paul Julien André Mauriat was born on 4 March 1925 in Marseilles, France. His father was a postal inspector who loved to play classical piano and violin. Mauriat began playing the piano between the age of three and four, and his father gave him music lessons when he was eight. In 1935, at the age of ten, he enrolled in the Conservatoire in Marseille to study classical music, but by the time he was 17, he had fallen in love with jazz and popular music.

At first, Mauriat followed in his father's footsteps and became a postman, but in 1942, when he was 17, he was hired as a dance band conductor. The band played in concert halls throughout Europe, though Mauriat remained based in Marseilles until 1958, when he moved to Paris. There, he became musical director for French singers, Charles Aznavour and Maurice Chevalier, touring with both of them. He arranged many of Aznavour's songs, including 'La Bohème', 'La Mamma', and 'Tu t'laisses aller', and stayed with him until the 1960s when his own recording career took off.

Mauriat released his first EP in 1957. Called *Paul Mauriat*, it was a four-track RGM release. One of his first songs, 'Rendez-vous au Lavandou', co-written with André Pascal, was awarded the 1958 le Coq d'or de la Chanson Française.

Between 1959 and 1964, as 'Paul Mauriat et Son Orchestre', he recorded several albums on Bel-Air. He wanted his recordings to reflect an international flavour, and to achieve this, he used various Anglo-Saxon-sounding names such as Richard Audrey and Willy Twist, the Greek-sounding Nico Papadopoulos, and the Italian-sounding Eduardo Ruo. He also recorded with Les Satellites, creating and arranging the vocal harmony backing their albums *Slow Rock And Twist* (Bel Air, 321 048, 10" LP, Mono, France 1961) and *Les Satellites Chantent Noel* (Bel Air 311.034, 10", LP, Mono, 1963). He also composed the music for French movies *Un Taxi Pour Tobrouk* (1961), *Horace 62* (1962) and *Faites Sauter La Banque* (1964)

It wasn't until 1967 that he achieved worldwide fame when he released the single, 'Love is Blue'. 'L'amour est bleu', written by Andre Popp and Pierre Cour, describes the pleasure and pain of love in colours. With its lush strings, Mauriat's arrangement owed more to Percy Faith than Ray Conniff. Sans vocals, it featured a harpsichord as its lead instrument. It was America's first instrumental number-one hit since 1963 and was France's only top-seller in the US. It was number one on the *Billboard* chart for 11 weeks and stayed on the chart for 27 weeks. It was originally the 1967 Eurovision Song Contest entry for Luxembourg by Greek singer Vicky Leandros (appearing as Vicky). While Leandros's version is pleasant enough, it didn't win the contest. The words are in French and so meant nothing to the English-speaking world. It plods along quite nicely without evoking any of the sentiments the lyrics suggest. However, in Paul Mauriat's hands, the tune – without its lyrics, but with lush strings and harpsichord – soars into the realms of high romance in an irresistibly catchy arrangement that seductively draws the listener in.

Mauriat went on to enjoy success worldwide with hit singles, EPs and numerous albums. He was particularly successful in Japan, where he sold over 15 million records. Completing over 25 concert tours there, he is the only international artist to play two sold-out shows on the same day at the famous Tokyo arena, Nippon Budokan.

He was also popular in Soviet Russia, where a number of his compositions were used in TV programmes and in cinema shorts such as the 1967 animated film, *Polygon*, *In The World Of Animals* and *Kinopanorama*. In their 1973 November issue, a monthly Soviet magazine, *Кругозор* (*Krugozor*) (1964 to 1992), included a set of six flexi 7" mono discs of Mauriat's music.

'Love Is Blue'

This stands as a pivotal moment in the evolution of easy listening music. The track begins with ethereal strings that create an otherworldly atmosphere, followed by a blend of woodwind and brass instruments that introduce the enchanting melody. The strings then envelop the composition, lending it a rich, harmonious texture. A brief interlude features the harpsichord, adding a touch of sophistication. As the woodwind section gracefully steps aside, the sharper tones of the brass instruments come to the forefront. This transition infuses the piece with a delightful contrast. The music captures a gentle, romantic ambience, encouraging lovers to embrace and sway tenderly in a slow, intimate dance.

Paul Mauriat died on 3 November 2006 in Perpignan, Pyrénées-Orientales, France.

Further Listening:

Listen Too! (Philips PHS-600-197) 1966
Of Vodka And Caviar (Philips PHS-600-215) 1967
From Paris With Love (Mercury/Wing SRW-16403) 1968
Blooming Hits: Paul Mauriat And His Orchestra (Philips PHS-600-248) 1968
More Mauriat (Philips PHS-600-226) 1968
Mauriat Magic (Philips PHS-600-270) 1968
Prevailing Airs (Philips PHS-600-280) 1968
Doing My Thing (Philips PHS-600-292) 1969
L.O.V.E. (Philips PHS-600-320) 1969
Let The Sunshine In/Midnight Cowboy/And Other Goodies (Philips PHS-600-337) 1969
Gone Is Love (Philips PHS-600-345) 1970

El Condor Pasa (Philips PHS-600-352) 1971
Theme From A Summer Place (MGM/Verve MV-5087) 1972
Love Theme From "The Godfather" (MGM SE-4838) 1972
Summer Memories (Philips 6332 109) [U.K. Import] 1972
Paul Mauriat 'Salutes The Beatles (Contour) 1972
A Taste Of France (Philips 6325 146) [Brazil Import] 1974
Have You Never Been Mellow? (MGM SE-4999) 1975
Plays The Hits Of Abba, Demis Roussos …(Power Exchange PXL023) [U.K. Import] 1977
Love Is Blue: Anniversary Collection (Featuring Zamfir on a pan flute) (CD Verve 834259-2) 1988
Love Is Blue: The Best Of Paul Mauriat (CD Polygram International 4101) 2000

Franck Pourcel

Key Recording: 'Only You (Loin De Vous)' b/w 'Rainy Night In Paris'

Released as a 7" 45 RPM Single
Label: Capitol Records
Release date: 1959

Franck Pourcel was born on 1 January 1913 in Marseilles, France. He was given his first name in tribute to the composer César Franck. His father was a technician but also a musician in the Navy in Marseilles. He began learning music at the age of six and was sent to study violin at the Conservatoire de Marseilles, where, at 16 years old, he received a First Prize. It was obvious he loved jazz more than classical music and, therefore, was allowed to study the drums. From there, he went to study at the Paris Conservatoire.

After completing his studies, he returned to Marseilles, where he worked in theatre and opera. He also played violin in a sextet and often played drums with other bands, performing in nightclubs and at dances. His dream, however, was to lead an orchestra of at least 50 musicians and to play big band music the way it was played in the US. He had an idea of the sound he wanted to create but, without an orchestra, was unable to do so. He became musical director of singers Yves Montand and Lucienne Boyer. With the latter, he toured in France and internationally for eight years.

His dream of conducting a large orchestra came true in 1952. But it wasn't his own orchestra and he could not play the music he loved. Deciding his future lay in America, he moved there. Getting a union card was not easy, nor was getting a start in the music business. He was given the opportunity to record in France and so he returned in 1953 to record an EP with his orchestra (Ducretet Thomson 460 V 075, 7", France), which included the tracks: 'Moulin Rouge', 'Limelight', 'La Valse Des Orgueilleux' and 'Swedish Rhapsody'. In 1956, he released another EP (Ducretet-Thomson Catalogue

460 V 239, EP, France). His records were selling well all over Europe, and he was conducting notable orchestras, such as the London Symphony Orchestra, the orchestra of the Société des Concerts du Conservatoire, the BBC London Orchestra at the Royal Festival Hall and the Concerts Lamoureux Orchestra at the Salle Pleyel. However, he believed that in order to achieve the worldwide fame that would enable him to create and maintain his own orchestra, he'd have to go back to America. 'At that time', he said, 'creating an orchestra with 50 musicians sounded nuts, but I wanted it. After many refusals, I moved [back] to the United States'.

In 1959, in the US, he recorded the 45 RPM that enabled him to fulfil his dreams: his easy listening rendition of The Platters' 1955 hit record, 'Only You' (Capitol F4165). 'Only You' was a huge worldwide hit, selling more than three million copies in the US alone, remaining on the *Billboard* charts for 16 weeks, and it launched Pourcel towards the career path he'd always dreamed of. He had, however, been billed on the record as 'Franck Pourcel And His French Fiddlers'. It was obviously a marketing ploy, but of it, he said, '… for me, the violin is the instrument closest to the human voice. I don't play it; I make it sing. It should be considered a vocal instrument, an instrument that speaks to the heart of man'. In Jazz and pop, the violin had largely been replaced by the guitar and the saxophone. Poulson was determined to reverse this trend and easy listening gave him his big opportunity to put the violin back where it belonged, at the heart of his arrangements, particularly in the form of lush strings.

He didn't like to record his own material, believing it not to be good enough. However, he, as J.W. Stole and Paul Mauriat as Del Roma, whose own recording career Pourcel helped launch, did write a hit record. It was 'Chariot'. It was a number one hit in France for Petula Clark Pye (7N I5522, 45", 1961), translated into English by Norman Gimbel as 'I Will Follow Him' (RCA Victor, 47-8139) and in 1963, it was a *Billboard* number one (three weeks) for 15-year-old Little Peggy March and stayed on the chart for 14 weeks.

In 1975, he was asked to compose an anthem for the Anglo/French supersonic jet Concorde, which he released on an eponymous album, *Concorde* (Pathe 2C066-15564). With its futuristic, not to mention quasi-disco (one of the tracks is 'Love Will Keep Us Together') sounding arrangements of the lead track and pop standards, it is considered a muzak/easy listening masterpiece.

Pourcel recorded over 250 albums. His last *Billboard* showing was in 1972 with a number 22 hit single, 'I Only Want To Say (Gethsemane)', from the rock opera *Jesus Christ Superstar*.

'Only You (Loin De Vue)'

We know Pourcel reintroduced violins to the realm of easy listening music with this rendition of 'Only You (Loin De Vue)'. The composition commences with a graceful string ensemble, crafting an ethereal atmosphere. Subtle notes sprinkle the arrangement, adding a touch of otherworldly charm. The melody unfurls as a blend of woodwinds and brass instruments takes centre stage while the strings provide a lush backdrop. A brief interlude of jazzy piano enhances the musical journey. The woodwinds gracefully recede, yielding the spotlight to the brassy section, which imparts a distinct, sharper resonance.

Pourcel's rendition of 'Only You (Loin De Vue)' evokes an irresistible desire for lovers to come together in an intimate embrace. As the music envelops them, their eyes share a tender, affectionate gaze, guiding them in a slow, romantic dance. Pourcel's artistry in this piece does indeed rekindle the allure of violins in the world of easy listening, adding a touch of French elegance to the genre.

Franck Pourcel died on 12 November 2000 in Neuilly-sur-Seine, France.

Further Listening:
Pourcel's Portraits (Capitol T-1855)
Les Baxter's "La Femme" (Frank Pourcel and His French Strings)
Our Man In Paris (Imperial LP-9304) 1965
Beautiful Obsession (Imperial LP-9322) 1966
Somewhere My Love (Imperial LP-9326) 1966
A Man And A Woman (Imperial LP-12343) 1967
Love Is Blue (Imperial LP-12383) 1968
Plays "Midnight Cowboy" (Paramount PAS-5015) 1969
Aquarius (Atco SD 33-299) 1969
Meets The Beatles (EMI 2C 062-11041-U) 1970
Theme From "Love Story" (Paramount PAS 5022) 1971
L'enfant Roi (EMI S URL 20-866) 1972
For All We Know (Paramount PAS 5035) 1972
Day By Day (Paramount PAS-6036) 1972
The World Is A Circle (Paramount PAS-6047) 1973
Plays Abba (EMI 10 C064-016.550) 1978
Hi-Fi 77: 20 Pop Instrumentals (EMI C-182-15570/71) (2) 1977
Digital Around The World (Odeon 064-073-551T) 1981
Golden Sounds Of Franck Purcel (CD Disky GS-864882) 1996
This Is Pourcel/The Cole Porter Story (CD EMI 7243-4-98147-2-1) 1999

Hugo Winterhalter

Key Recording: The Eyes Of Love

Released as a Vinyl LP
Side A: 'With My Eyes Wide Open I'm Dreaming' (Revel, Gordon)/'I'll See You Again' (Noel Coward)/'There's Danger In Your Eyes, Cherie!' (Richman, Meskill, Welding)/'Star Eyes' (Don Raye, Gene De Paul)/'I'll Be Seeing You' (Irving Kahal, Sammy Fain)/'I Only Have Eyes For You' (Al Dubin, Harry Warren)
Side B: 'The Eyes Of Love' (Hugo Winterhalter)/'Green Eyes' (Utrera, Rivera,

Woods, Menendez)/'See It My Way' (Carmen Vitale, Robert Melin)/'Smoke Gets In Your Eyes' (Jerome Kern, Otto Harbach)/'I See Faces Before Me' (Arthur Schwartz – Harold Dietz)/'Your Eyes Have Told Me So' (Van Alstyne, Kahn, Blaufuss)
Label: RCA
Release date: 1957

Hugo Winterhalter was born in Wilkes-Barre, Pennsylvania, on 15 August 1909 to Hugo Winterhalter and Mary Gallagher, both second-generation German Americans. He studied music at Mount St. Mary's in Emmitsburg, Maryland and graduated with a diploma in 1931. He had been a member of the orchestra, showcasing his saxophone skills, and sang in two choirs. Upon leaving Mount St Mary's, he continued his musical education, focusing on the violin and reed instruments at the New England Conservatory of Music.

After completing his studies, he started a career in education and spent several years teaching. However, his passion for music eventually led him to turn professional in the mid-1930s, cutting his teeth working as a sideman and arranger for the likes of Count Basie, Tommy Dorsey, Raymond Scott, Claude Thornhill and others. He went on to map out a fruitful career arranging and conducting music for renowned vocalists like Dinah Shore and Billy Eckstine. His journey in the music industry took a significant turn in 1948 when he assumed the role of musical director at MGM Records. Two years later, he moved to Columbia Records, where he achieved chart success with hits like 'Jealous Heart' and 'Blue Christmas'.

In 1950, Winterhalter made another career move, this time to RCA Victor. There, he arranged music for a host of popular chart-topping artists, including Perry Como, Harry Belafonte, Eddie Fisher, Jaye P. Morgan and The Ames Brothers. He also ventured into recording instrumental albums, producing the pioneering collection of TV theme songs *The Great Music Themes Of Television* in 1952. His career was marked by several chart-toppers like 'Mr. Touchdown, U.S.A.' (RCA Victor 473913), 'A Kiss to Build a Dream On' (RCA Victor 47-4455), 'The Magic Tango' (RCA Victor 47-5769) and 'Blue Christmas' (Columbia 38635).

Collaborating with pianist Eddie Heywood, he achieved a minor hit with 'Land Of Dreams' in 1954, but two years later, he hit the top of the *Billboard* chart with the easy listening classic 'Canadian Sunset', selling over a million copies and, thereby, earning a gold disc from the RIAA (Recording Industry Association of America).

By now, Winterhalter was fitting neatly into an easy listening mode of making music. While not exactly an inventor of easy listening, his arrangements were characterised by an innate talent for creating lush, sophisticated orchestrations that evoked a sense of serenity and charm, along with an ability to take popular songs and transform them into dreamy, accessible compositions, particularly with pieces like the title song of the album above, and 'Blue Tango' and 'The Little Shoemaker', which were emblematic of his soothing and polished sound. Such tracks became staples on radio stations and in households among his many dedicated followers. This alone qualifies him to stand beside the likes of Mantovani and Percy Faith in the panoply of easy listening heroes, if not entirely as their equal (as if that really matters!)

Remaining with RCA Victor until 1963, Winterhalter then moved to Kapp. During his time at Kapp, he recorded several albums, including *The Best Of '64* and its sequel *The Big Hits Of 1965*, before turning his focus towards Broadway. He explored opportunities in television and occasionally contributed to album projects for various budget labels. His final appearance on the US music charts came in 1969 with the release of 'Theme From 'Popi'' on Musicor Records (1368), a single that reached the 35th spot on the *Billboard* Easy Listening Top 40 chart.

'The Eyes Of Love'

As with all the tracks on this album, 'The Eyes Of Love' offers a lush interpretation of easy listening music. The composition commences with ethereal strings and subtle notes, creating an otherworldly atmosphere. A piano introduces the melody, with strings enriching the overall harmony. The strings again gracefully retreat, yielding the spotlight to the piano and woodwind. This track exudes an enchanting allure, inviting couples to share an intimate, slow dance in each other's arms. Winterhalter's rendition of easy listening music is a captivating blend of musical elements, creating a sensuous and romantic ambience.

Hugo Winterhalter died on 17 September 1973 in Greenwich, Connecticut, USA.

Further Listening:

Hugo Winterhalter...goes Latin (RCA LSP-1677) 1957
Wish You Were Here (RCA LSP-1904) 1959
Two Sides Of Winterhalter (RCA LSP-1905) 1959
Hugo Winterhalter Goes...Hawaiian (RCA LSP-2417) 1962
Hugo Winterhalter Goes...Continental (RCA LSP-2482) 1963
I Only Have Eyes For You (RCA LSP-2645) 1964
The Best Of Winterhalter (RCA LSP-3379[e]) 1965
Saturday Night At The Movies (Musico MDS-1001)
Motion Picture Hit Themes (Musico MDS-1040)
Your Favourite Motion Picture Music (Musicor M2S-3178) [2]
Classical Gas (with Eddie Heywood) (Musicor MS-32170)
Love Story (Musicor MS-3196) 1972
16 Beautiful Hits (CD Deluxe DCD-7901) 1994
The Eyes Of Love (CD Good Music DMC2-1420) 1996 [2]
The Very Best Of Hugo Winterhalter (CD Taragon TARCD-1080) 2000

Acker Bilk

Key Recording: 'Stranger On The Shore'

Released as a 7" 45 RPM Single
Label: Columbia
Release date: 1962

Bernard Stanley Bilk was born on 28 January 1929 in Pensford, Somerset. He appears to have acquired the nickname 'Acker', quite early in life and it stuck. Acker is Somerset slang for 'friend or 'mate'. As a young boy, he was encouraged to learn the piano at home but found it got in the way of his first love, football. For three years after leaving school, he worked in a cigarette factory, before being called up for national service in the Royal Engineers. A friend is said to have given him a beaten-up old clarinet bought in a bazaar in the Suez Canal Zone, where they were both stationed. Getting interested in making it work, Bilk made a reed for it himself. Later, he borrowed a better clarinet from the army and taught himself to play it.

On being demobbed and keeping the clarinet he'd borrowed, he trained as a blacksmith in Bristol while playing in local jazz bands. He moved to London to play in the trad jazz scene there but didn't like it and returned to his hometown, where he formed his own band, which eventually came to be called the Paramount Jazz Band. In 1951, an agent got them a six-week booking in a bierkeller in Dusseldorf, playing seven hours a night, seven nights a week. It was then that Bilk perfected his distinctive clarinet playing style. It was due, he claimed, to losing his front teeth in a school fight and half a finger in a sledging accident. It was also in Dusseldorf that Bilk and his band adopted what was to become their distinctive dress code: striped waistcoats, ties and bowler hats.

Trad jazz was booming in England and on his return, Bilk knew he'd have to base himself in London if he was to make a career out of performing. He cut a single, 'Summer Set' (Columbia DB-4382), penned by himself and pianist Dave Collett. A pun on his home county, it got to number five on the UK Singles Chart.

While ostensibly a jazz musician, in 1961, Bilk produced what is perhaps the moodiest of all smooth, easy listening tunes, 'A Stranger On The Shore'. Originally called 'Jenny' for his daughter of the same name, Bilk changed the tune's name to that of a TV series in which it was going to feature as the theme music. Played in what was by now his breathy, irresistibly moody vibrato style, the record was a huge hit on both sides of the Atlantic, peaking at number two and staying on the English charts for 55 weeks. Furthermore, it stayed at number one on the US *Billboard* charts for seven weeks and then remained on the chart for another 21 weeks, earning a gold record. Bilk was only the second UK artist to have a number-one hit on the US *Billboard* charts, the first being war-time sweetheart Vera Lynn, in 1952 with 'Auf Wiedersehn Sweetheart'.

Trad jazz in the UK was eclipsed by the arrival of skiffle and rock 'n' roll, but remained popular on the club and cabaret scene, where Acker Bilk and his

Paramount Jazz Band remained much in demand. He continued to make top-selling EPs and albums such as *A Taste Of Honey* (Columbia SCX 3469, UK, 1963) and *Mood For Love* (ATCO SD 33-1971, US, 1966), covering classic easy listening songs and, as you'd expect, hits of the day. Backed by a string ensemble – often the Leon Young String Ensemble – his arrangements were on par with anything put out by Mantovani and Percy Faith, making them timeless easy listening gems.

Collaborating with Danish jazz pianist and composer Bent Fabricius-Bjerre – better known as Bent Fabrik – and calling themselves Mr Acker Bilk and Bent Fabrik, Bilk enjoyed further success in the US in 1965 with an album called *Together* (ATCO 33-175). In 1976, he had a UK number five hit with 'Aria', another timeless tune played in his inimitable breathy style.

His last UK album success was in 1978 with *Evergreen* (Pye PW5045, Warwick PW 5045), a collection of pop standards, including contemporary hits such as 'Feelings', 'You Light Up My Life', 'Don't It Make My Brown Eyes Blue', 'My Sweet Lord', 'Help Me Make It Through The Night', 'When I Need You', 'Yesterday' and 'When A Child Is Born'.

'Stranger On The Shore' was included on the soundtrack of *Sweet Dreams*, the 1985 Hollywood biopic of Patsy Cline's life and times.

'Stranger On The Shore'

'Stranger On The Shore' is the epitome of smooth, easy listening music. The song commences with delicate strings, evoking an otherworldly atmosphere. Gradually, Bilk's signature clarinet introduces a captivating melody. As the song progresses, the strings enrich the musical tapestry, adding an extra layer of charm. Then, the string section gracefully recedes, making way for the sharper, more pronounced tones of Bilk's clarinet to again take centre stage. This dynamic shift in instrumentation creates a harmonious balance that is both soothing and captivating. 'Stranger On The Shore' is a masterpiece in the realm of easy listening music, inviting you to lose yourself in its mellowness and timeless allure.

Acker Bilk died on 2 November 2014 in Bath, Somerset, UK.

Further Listening:

Stranger On The Shore (Metronome B-1492), 1961
Above The Stars (Atco Records SD 33-144) 1962
Lansdowne Folio (Columbia 33SX1348) 1962

Herb Alpert

Key Recording: The Lonely Bull

Released as a Vinyl LP
Tracklist:
A-side: 'The Lonely Bull (El Solo Toro)' (Sol Lake)/'El Lobo (The Wolf)' (Harry Green, Sol Lake)/'Tijuana Sauerkraut' (Herb Alpert, Jerry Moss)/'Deasfinado'

(Antônio Carlos Jobim, Newton Mendonca)/'Mexico' (Boudleaux Bryant)/'Never On Sunday' (Manos Hadjidakis, Billy Towne)
B-side: 'Struttin' With Maria' (Herb Alpert)/'Let It Be Me' (Gilbert Bécaud, Mann Curtis, Pierre Delanoë)/'Acapulco 1922' (Dave Alpert (As Eldon Allan))/'Limbo Rock' (Billy Strange)/'Crawfish' (Sol Lake, Elsa Doran)/'A Quiet Tear (Lágrima Quieta)' (Herb Alpert)
Label: A&M Records
Release date: 1962

Herb Alpert was born on 31 March 1935 in Los Angeles, California, US. The younger of two sons, he was born into a Jewish immigrant family of musicians, his father from Ukraine and his mother from Romania. His father, while working as a tailor, was an accomplished mandolin player and his mother taught violin. Alpert's younger brother, David, took up the drums, and he took up the trumpet, both at very young ages.

In 1952, he joined the US Army, performing regularly at ceremonial events, before studying at the University of Southern California's Thornton School of Music, playing trumpet in the university's Trojan Marching Band. In 1957, he teamed up with Rob Weerts and together they wrote a number of Top 20 hits, not least 'Baby Talk' by Jan and Dean and 'Wonderful World' by Sam Cooke. In 1960, he began his recording career as a vocalist at RCA Records under the name of Dore Alpert. Next, he teamed up with Jerry Moss and in 1962, they formed their own record label: the famed and highly successful A&M Records. It was a slow beginning, with Alpert's garage doubling as a recording studio.

Albert created his unique sound after being inspired by a visit to a bullfight in Tijuana, Mexico, where he watched the spectators being thoroughly roused by a mariachi band of brass musicians. He set out to recreate the sound in a pop record. In his home garage recording studio, he took a song written by Sole Lake called 'Twinkle Star', overdubbed its intro with the sound of cheering bullfight spectators and added wordless female singers, while playing a slightly out-of-sync smooth trumpet solo. Changing its name to 'The Lonely Bull' (AM 8051), it gave him a Top Ten hit in 1962. An album of the same name quickly followed, which peaked at number six on the *Billboard* album charts. He had financed and distributed the record himself, giving A&M Records its best possible start in the music business. Alpert went on to have numerous hit singles and albums, featuring more compositions by Sole Lake and covering, in his Mexican-mariachi sound, hit songs of the day.

Dispensing with lush strings and replacing them with brass, particularly his own trumpet, drums and guitars, Alpert is often described as the godfather of Latin easy listening. His music continued the easy listening tradition of creating a romantic mood and atmosphere, but in a completely different way, a way that is distinctly south of the US-Mexican border. He also covered pop standards. In 1965, he released another two albums on A&M: *Whipped Cream & Other Delights* (SP-4110, US) and *!!Going Places!!* (SP-4112). They were amongst A&M's best-selling albums, tracks from which were given a lot of airtime on the radio. 'A Taste of Honey' from *Whipped Cream*, which was an easy listening chart number one for five weeks, won a Grammy Award. He continued to enjoy Top Five and Top Ten hits through the 60s. In 1966, he and his band sold over 13 million records, even out-selling The Beatles that year.

As a vocalist in 1968, he had a smash hit with 'This Guy's In Love With You' (A&M 929, US). The song, in fact, written and arranged by Burt Bacharach and Hal David, was originally intended to be the theme music to a television series, but Alpert was persuaded to release it as a single and it topped *Billboard*'s pop charts and remained on the chart overall for 17 weeks. He and his band continued to have hit records up until 1975. He had another number-one pop hit in 1979 with the instrumental, 'Rise' (A&M 2151, US). As a vocalist, he continued to have Top Ten and Top 40 hits through the 80s, his last chart entry (number 21 in 1987) being 'Making Love In The Rain' (A&M 2949, 45 RPM, US).

Herb Alpert also painted and sculpted, exhibiting in Beverley Hills, California in 2010 and 2013.

From the sample of tracks below, it is obvious, as it is with all the great arrangers in our genre, that Alpert is driven by what he knew. He's a trumpeter and the solo trumpet dominates all his recordings. Add to this his abilities in the studio and you start to understand where his ideas came from. 'The Lonely Bull', for example, is a mixture of trumpets but famously, as discussed above, with a Latin vibe added. There is also a nod to his childhood influences, his father being an accomplished mandolin player, an instrument that is heard in many of his arrangements. There is also the occasional addition of jazz and classical guitars, played cleanly, with that Latin feel always there.

'The Lonely Bull'

The song opens with the cheering of a crowd at a bullfight before the brass comes in with full gusto, dramatically announcing the beginning of the dual about to take place between the bull and toreador. Albert is setting the scene. Then, a jazzy, clean lead guitar enters. It is most likely a hollow-bodied electric guitar popular in jazz and blues at the time and is used to add a softer tone. This is supported by swing percussion and brief staccato notes from a mandolin, followed by the entrance of a 'wordless' choir, introducing dynamics and variety. Brass builds towards the end of the track to signify that the dual is coming to an end, and we hear the joyous cheers of the crowd, indicating that the poor, lonely bull of the title was not the victor. Where is the romance in this song? Well, in the context of man meets woman, there isn't any. It's a sign of things to come, for what we have instead is the disturbing act of man against beast for the purposes of entertainment. Depending on your disposition, you will either cheer along with the crowd as the toreador triumphs or be saddened, perhaps horrified, at the inhumane fate of the bull. A song that is as reflective as it is moody.

'EL Lobo (The Wolf)'

This is an extraordinarily dramatic song which opens with swing percussion and singular bass notes from a clean jazz guitar, before a classical guitar picks up the melody, with all three then playing together. Trumpets follow to take over the lead on the melody, creating a terrible sense of foreboding. A 'voiceless' choir sighs, before the addition of equally doleful mandolin trills, while the classical guitar returns, introducing a touch of variation, followed by a melancholic piano and the mournful return of trumpets. The track ends with a wailing, questioning trumpet solo, as tubular bells solemnly drift away. There is romance here, but it is as full of an overstatement as you'd expect from a Latin-American mix. Your heart breaks, but for whom or what? It can't be for the wolf in the title; it has to be, surely, for the woman left behind with her children, as her husband, perhaps a bandito, or maybe a revolutionary, goes off to fulfil his destiny; she fears never to return.

Herb Alpert is still alive and performing.

Further Listening:

The Lonely Bull (A&M Records – SP-4101) 1962
South Of The Border (A&M Records – SP 4108) 1964
Whipped Cream & Other Delights (A&M Records – SP 4110) 1965
Going Places (A&M Records SP-4112) 1965
The Beat Of The Brass (A&M Records SP-4146) 1968
Christmas Album (A&M Records SP 4166) 1968
Warm (Herb Alpert Presents 70205) 1969
Summertime (A&M Records SP-4314) 1971
You Smile – The Song Begins (A&M Records SP 3639) 1974
Just You And Me (A&M SP 4592) 1976
Rise (A&M Records MFSL 1-053) 1979

Sergio Mendez

Key Recording: Herb Alpert Presents Sergio Mendez And Brazil '66

Released as a Vinyl LP
Tracklist:
A-Side: 'Mais Que Nada (Ma-sh Kay Nada)' (Jorge Ben)/'One Note Samba'/'Spanish Flea' (Carlos Jobin, Newton Mendoca, Julius Wechter)/'The Joker' (Anthony Newley, Lesley Bricusse)/'Going Out Of My Head' (Bobby Weinstein, Teddy Randazzo)/'Tim Dom Dom (Chim Dome Dome)' (Coda, Joao Mello)
B-Side: 'Day Tripper' (Lennon, McCartney)/'Agua De Beber (Agwa Gee Beberr)' (Antoniop Carlos Jobim, Norman, Gimbel, Vinicius de Moraes)/'Slow Hot Wind' (Henry Mancini, Norman Gimbel)/'O Pato (O Pawtoo)' (Jayme Silva, Neuza Teixeira)/'Berimbau (Ber-im-bough)' (Baden Powell, Norman Gilbert, Vinicius de Moraes)

Label: A&M Records
Release date: 1966

Sergio Mendez was born on 11 February 1941 in Niteroi, Brazil, the son of a physician. He attended the local conservatory with hopes of becoming a classical pianist. However, his interest in jazz grew and in the 1950s, he started playing in nightclubs. He began playing with Antônio Carlos Jobim and the many US jazz musicians who were touring Brazil. In 1961, he formed his own sextet, Bossa Rio – the bossa nova, a jazzy derivative of samba, was gaining popularity – and in 1961, they released *Dance Moderno* (Phillips 630.491 L, Brazil). The band, consisting of two trombones, tenor saxophone, bass, drums, and piano, began to tour Europe and the United States, playing in the US at the famed Birdland and Carnegie Hall. He recorded albums with Julian 'Cannonball' Adderley and Herbie Mann. In 1964, he settled permanently in the US, where, alongside Sergio Mendes and Brazil '65, he recorded two albums with Atlantic Records and then Capitol Records. These recordings weren't a great success outside of Southern California and Mendes decided upon a new line-up:

> I ran into the idea of having two girls singing – don't ask me why – I just liked that sound. Then I decided to work with not only Brazilian songs but well-known English-language songs by composer, Burt Bacharach, and The Beatles. For me, the song and the melody are everything. So, we started working on getting those great songs put into a Brazilian pocket. We would work all day long, break for lunch and we would go back and try an assortment of different rhythms, so it was like a workshop. It was wonderful.

Sergio Mendes had found his new sound. He left Capitol Records and went to Herb Alpert's A&M Records, where he recorded his hit album *Sergio Mendes and Brazil '66*.

What Herb Alpert had started in terms of Latin easy listening was fully established worldwide by Mendes with his hit album *Herb Albert Presents Sergio Mendez and Brazil '66*. Albert himself played no small part in the production of the music on the album. With his name added to its title, he guaranteed it would grab people's attention. My namesake, The Beatles press officer, Derek Taylor, wrote in the sleeve notes to the album that Sergio Mendes had created 'with considerable taste, a delicate blend of piano jazz, subtle Latin undertones, with borrowings from Lennon and McCartney and Mancini'. Although Mendez uses a mixture of wordless and lyric-singing female voices singing in English and Portuguese, the vocals are more part of the instrumentation than anything that might be called a lead vocal. The music itself is stylishly seductive, with catchy arrangements of a bosa nova rhythm on top of Mendes's piano playing. There is a cover of The Beatles' 'Day Tripper' and two Henri Mancini songs. 'Mas Que Nada', the album's opening track, reached number four on the US *Billboard* charts and stayed on the chart for 17 weeks.

Touring with Herb Alpert and The Tijuana Brass, Sergio Mendes and Brazil '66 very quickly gained worldwide fame. Mendes continued to enjoy chart success. In 1968, he had a number-two hit with a Latin-cool cover of 'The Look Of Love' (A&M 924), which stayed on the chart for 18 weeks, and a number-one hit with a similarly cool cover of The Beatles' song, 'Fool On The Hill', which stayed on the chart for 15 weeks. He also had a number-two hit with Simon and Garfunkel's (original arrangement by Martin Carthy) 'Scarborough Fair'. Latin dance had become listenable, more than simply danceable, and very easily began to slot into the easy listening mode. More Top 20 and 40 hits followed right up until 1987, the final 45 rpm being 'What Do We Mean To Each Other?' (A&M 2917, US) which reached number 18 on the *Billboard* chart.

In the samples described below, it can be seen how Latin America meets North American mood music on this album, with its combination of female vocals and overall harmonies, samba percussion and piano. There are some very well-known songs, from 'Mas Que Nada' to The Beatles' classic, 'Day Tripper'. It is likely Mendes' covering of 'Day Tripper' and 'Fool On The Hill' had some influence on the Buena Vista Club band, formed in 1996 in Havana, Cuba, in their collaborations with the likes of Coldplay, Kaiser Chiefs and Maroon 5, covering some of their most iconic tracks with a similar Latin American feel.

The mix of lead vocals singing in unison, before breaking into male and female harmonics and choral-like vocals, helps to add colour to each track, as well as serving to distinguish between different parts of the song. The vocals are backed by an array of Latin American percussive instruments, which are then expertly joined by a jazz/blues piano delivering major triad and major/minor 7th and 9th chords, with solos being built around the major and minor pentatonic scales. These techniques together deliver the samba feel that runs throughout the album. Added to this and helping to deliver a big sound without the benefit of the conventional easy listening orchestra, was the use of modern recording techniques.

'Mas Que Nada'

This song opens with piano and Latin percussion delivered mainly from the cymbals, clave (Woodblock), timbales and, right at the back of the mix, a wooden slide whistle, with the vocal harmony singing the melody before the female vocal takes the lead. The female vocal takes the lead throughout, with the male vocal contributing a choral dimension that interweaves with the melody, offering moments of contrast. Meanwhile, the rhythm section, comprised of piano and percussion, propels the song forward. The song finishes with a blues/jazz piano solo, choral harmonies replacing, what is normally in easy listening music arrangements, the string section. It is the bubbly, uplifting samba arrangement that delivers the urge to bring a sexy rhythm to life. The romantic feel of the song is more subtle than normal; its exotic rhythms would suggest to the more sophisticated couple that there is more to lovemaking than, well, just lovemaking.

'One Note Samba'/'Spanish Flea'

As in the track before, percussion and piano start with female vocal harmony leading to a single female lead, before a combined female and male chorus returns with shared tweet, tweet, tweedled dos and bob, bobs bombs etc. It is the female lead and mixed vocal harmonies that give the arrangement its uplifting momentum. Where the romance comes in is up to each listener to decide in their own sweet or otherwise, way.

'Day Tripper'

The track opens with the guitar riff made famous by The Beatles but here given a Latin American piano vibe, before the lyric is delivered, again, by two females singing in unison. It is in this song that you find it easiest to see how some of the tone and feel of this album is delivered. It is not only through the arrangement of instruments, chorus and lead vocals but the technical expertise of the producer and sound engineer. The female chorus shifts from the left stereo channel to the right and back again and in an almost illusory way. The big, rounded, full sound, which normally takes a whole orchestra to create, is delivered here in the way the instruments are mixed, with the piano playing back through the right channel and the rhythm section, percussion and bass taking the left, with the female vocals playing back as described above, while the male vocals are shared equally between left and right channels. In this way, as big a sound is created as was created by, for example, Paul Weston, Jackie Gleason and Mantovani using a full orchestra. Romance has fled here to be replaced by anger, regret and disillusion.

Sergio Mendes is still alive and active.

Further Listening:

Cannonball's Bossa Nova (Riverside/Capitol Records ST-2877) 1962
Do The Bossa Nova With Herbie Mann, Latin Fever with Herbie Mann (Fresh Sound Records ABS 137258) 1962
Você Ainda Não Ouviu Nada! (a.k.a., The Beat of Brazil) (Philips P632701L) 1963
The Swinger From Rio (a.k.a., Bossa Nova York) (Atlantic AL33144) 1964
In Person At El Matador (Atlantic SAL 933284) 1965
Brasil '65 (a.k.a. In The Brazilian Bag) (Capitol T 2294) 1965
Equinox (A&M SP 4122) 1967
Quiet Nights (Philips PHS 600-263) 1967
Fool On The Hill (A&M SPX 4160) 1968
Crystal Illusions (A&M AMLS 948) 1969
Ye-Me-Lê (A&M SP-4236) 1969

Henri Mancini

Key Recording: Moon River From The Soundtrack To Breakfast At Tiffany's (Music From The Motion Picture Score)

Released as a Vinyl LP
Label: RCA
Release date: 1961

Enrico Nicola Mancini was born on 16 April 1924 in Cleveland, Ohio, US to Italian parents, Quinto and Anna Pece Mancini, who had immigrated to the US from the Abruzzo region of Southern-eastern Italy. While not ostensibly an easy listening composer or bandleader, he wrote some wonderful, timeless tunes that easy listening band leaders and their fans took to their hearts. He grew up in Aliquippa, a small town in Beaver County, Pennsylvania. His father was a steelworker and played music in an orchestra of the Order of the Sons of Italy. Recognising his son's musical talents from a very early age, he encouraged him to play the flute and the piano, wanting his son to become a music teacher. In later years, Mr Mancini would recall going to the movies with his father to see Cecil B. DeMille's epic, *The Crusades*. His imagination was fired by Rudolph Kopp's soundtrack and he decided, he later said, that despite his father's wishes, he was going to write film scores.

At school, he played in his High School Orchestra. After graduating, he joined the music school at the Carnegie Institute of Technology in Pittsburgh, where he studied under Max Adkins, who was conductor of the 25-piece Stanley Theatre Orchestra. Adkins led the orchestra from 1939 and was a brilliant saxophonist and clarinettist who had many offers to go on the road with big bands but preferred to stay at home close to his family in Pittsburgh. Mancini could not have had a better mentor. He was noted as one of the best teachers of reed instruments on the East Coast and gave refresher lessons to touring musicians. As well as Mancini, he taught a number of other great musicians, including Billy Strayhorn, Jerry Fielding and Bud Estes. He was also a noted arranger, much in demand to write for such giants of the jazz big band era as Alvino Ray, Jimmy Dorsey and others. In his autobiography, *Did They Mention The Music?*, Mancini thanked Adkins for being 'the most important influence on his life'.

Mancini next studied at New York's Juilliard School. However, his studies were interrupted when he was called up to fight in World War II, where he served in both the Army Air Forces and the infantry. His own career in show business was launched when Adkins introduced him to Benny Goodman, saying, 'I'd like this kid to do an arrangement for you'. Goodman liked what he heard and Mancini never looked back. At the end of the war, he was recruited by Tex Beneke, who had taken over the leadership of the late Glen Miller band. However, with the passing of the big band era and his burning ambition to write film scores, Mancini moved to Hollywood in the early 1950s.

Writing music first for radio shows, he became a staff composer for Universal-International studios in the early days and wrote music for scenes in movies like *Abbott And Costello Meet Dr. Jekyll And Mr. Hyde, Creature From The Black Lagoo* and *Ma And Pa Kettle At Home*. He also contributed music to one of Hollywood's first rock musicals, *Rock, Pretty Baby*. His background in the jazz music of the big band era led him to take a new approach to film score composition, which, up until then, had been mainly symphonic and heavily orchestrated. Moviemaking was changing and a more modern approach was called for.

In 1958, he wrote the score for a new television detective series, *Peter Gunn*. It was revolutionary and was, series producer Blake Edwards said, as much as anything, responsible for the series' huge success. Mancini said he 'used a guitar and piano in unison to achieve [the desired] sinister effect with some frightened saxophones and shouting brass'. Ray Anthony and his Orchestra, with the emphasis on a throbbing guitar riff and a wailing saxophone, took the main theme into the Top Ten *Billboard* chart in January 1959, and in the following June, rock 'n' roll guitarist Duane Eddy had a worldwide hit with a purely rock/R&B arrangement.

Peter Gunn, however, was no easy listening hit. But what Mancini produced next undoubtedly was. It was the music to the 1961 Blake Edward's film *Breakfast At Tiffany's,* which included one of easy listening's moodiest ever songs, 'Moon River'. Johnny Mercer wrote the words and Henri Mancini wrote the music. They won the year's Oscar for Best Original Song and Mancini himself won an Oscar for Best Original Score. Of the music, *Time* magazine said Mancini 'sets off his melodies with a walking bass, extends them with choral and string variations and varies them with the brisk sounds of combo jazz. 'Moon River' is sobbed by a plaintive harmonica, repeated by strings, hummed and then sung by the chorus, finally resolved with the harmonica again'.

Famously sung in the film by Audrey Hepburn, Robert Wright perceptively said in 'The Atlantic Monthly' that 'Moon River' is 'a love sung [sic] to wanderlust. Or a romantic song in which the romantic partner is the idea of romance'. So, it's not exactly a romantic love song. Yet it is so full of a romantic yearning, in fact, for a childhood idyl as might have been known by John Mercer, who grew up in America's Deep South, that it could easily be a song about lost love between a man and a woman. This, in reality, is what most people do, in fact, think the song is about.

Jerry Butler had a number 11 *Billboard* pop chart hit with 'Moon River' in December 1961, and a number three rating in the new Easy Listening chart. Mancini released his own instrumental version of it a few weeks later, reaching the same chart positions. While his version did not feature a vocalist singing the lyric, he did include a 'wordless' chorus and soaring strings, giving it an unmistakable easy listening identity. Danny Williams took it to number one in the UK charts in the same year. All the greats, from Mantovani to James Last, and everyone in between, have recorded it, giving it their own distinctive treatments, but never leaving out the strings.

'Moon River' is beaten only by The Beatles' 'Yesterday' in being the most recorded song in pop history. Mancini scored another easy listening hit when his arrangement of Nito Roso's tune to Franco Zeffirelli's film *Romeo and Juliette* hit the number-one spot on *Billboard*'s Easy Listening chart and stayed there for eight weeks. It reached number one on the pop chart, where it stayed for two weeks, ending The Beatles' five-week run with 'Get Back'.

'Moon River'

Label: Crown Records

Release date: 1964

This instrumental version, rather than the film version, effortlessly captures the essence of the American South's laid-back lifestyle. The song starts with a walking double bass accompanied by the single chords of a banjo, creating an enchanting atmosphere throughout. A sprinkling of notes adds an ethereal touch, setting the stage for a seamless blend of woodwind and brass instruments, which introduce the heartwarming melody. As the song progresses, the strings gracefully enhance the musical landscape, as a vocal chorus singing Mercer's lyrics makes a charming appearance. The woodwind section gracefully recedes, allowing the brighter, more resonant brass instruments to take the spotlight. The result is a harmonious balance, inviting you to embrace your loved one and sway gently in a slow, affectionate dance.

'Moon River' is a musical masterpiece, not least of all because of Johnny Mercer's evocative lyrics reminding one of the world of Mark Twain's all-American masterpiece *Huckleberry Finn*.

Henri Mancini died on 14 June 1994 in Los Angeles, California, USA.

Further Listening:

Driftwood And Dreams (Liberty LRP-3049) 1957
Uniquely Mancini (LSP-2692) 1963
"Dear Heart" And Other Songs About Love (LSP-26990) 1965
Music Of Hawaii (LSP-3713) 1966
Mancini '67 (LSP-3694) 1967
Two For The Road (LSP-3802) 1967
A Warm Shade Of Ivory (LSP-4140) 1969
Six Hours Past Sunset (LSP-4239) 1969
Mancini Country (LSP-4307) 1970
Theme From "Z" And Other Film Music (LSP-4350) 1970
Plays The Theme From "Love Story" (LSP-4466) 1971
Brass On Ivory (LSP-4629) 1972
Brass, Ivory, And Strings (RCA 0098) 1973
Plays Those Evergreen Classics (Reader's Digest RDS 9959) 1982

Sunflower: Original soundtrack (CD Avco Embassy 11001) 1987
Film Favorites (CD BMG 295, 469) 1990
Cinema Italiano (CD RCA 60706-2-RC) 1990

General Select Discography

Apart from the prolifically available recordings of the masters of Easy Listening music, there are numerous minor band leaders and composers, some of whom might be described as 'one-hit wonders' and 'also-rans', but who, nevertheless, were heralded and loved by their spell-bound fans. I have included several of them in this discography simply because they are well worth seeking out. There are others, such as the 101 Strings, whose commercially packaged budget-priced success can only be described as phenomenal, although they had little chart success. They are also included in this discography.

Original Early Muzak Transcriptions Transferred To Reel-To-Reel Tape

Muzak recordings are not designed to be sold commercially to the public and are, therefore, not readily available in the usual retail outlets. Thanks to the internet, however, recordings can be found and downloaded. As has already been said above, some of muzak's band leaders and session men were relatively well-known in music and recording circles and only recorded for Muzak to supplement their meagre incomes. Other bands and orchestras were created and named for specific recording sessions and then as quickly, ceased to exist outside of those recording sessions. They may have been heard by millions of people as background music in public places but were seldom if ever, noted or known for these recordings. Transcriptions of these early recordings can be found in the Muzak section of The Internet Archive.

Commercial Recordings

101 Strings

Cited above in 'Overview', their albums are well worth listening to, as is attested to by their multi-million sales.

Grand Canyon Suite (Somerset SF-7900) 1950
Caribbean Cruise (as the Rio Carnival Orchestra) (Somerset P-5900) 1959
The Soul Of Spain (Somerset SF-6600) 1959
Gypsy Camp Fires (Somerset SF-8100) 1960
Back Beat Symphony (Somerset P-11500)
Hawaiian Paradise (Somerset SF-12800) 1961
I Love Paris (Somerset SF-13000) 1962
Play The World's Great Standards (Stereo Fidelity SF-4300)
Million Seller Songs Of The Sixties (Stereo Fidelity SF-21300) 1963
Songs Of The Seasons In Japan (Alshire S-5019) 1964
Mood Vienna (Alshire S-5023) 1965
The Quiet Hours (Alshire S-5026) 1965
East Of Suez (Alshire S-5027) 1965

Italia Con Amore (From Italy With Love) (Alshire S-5030) 1965
The Soul Of Mexico (Alshire S-5032) 1966
Fly Me To The Moon (Alshire S-5033) 1966
A Romantic Mood For Dining And Dreaming (Alshire S-5034) 1966
Sounds And Songs Of The Jet Set (Alshire S-5043) 1967
The Soul Of Greece (Alshire S-5047) 1967
101 Strings Play Million Seller Hits Of 1966 (With Don Costa) (Alshire S-5050) 1967
Swingin' Things (Scored By Don Costa) (Alshire S-5055) 1967
Sounds Of Today (Alshire S-5078) 1968
Million Seller Hits Written By The Beatles And Other "Now Writers" (Alshire S-5111) 1968
Astro-Sounds: From Beyond The Year 2000 (Alshire S-5119) 1968
African Safari (Alshire S-5171) 1969
More Hits Songs Of Today's Charts (Alshire S-5175) 1969
Million Seller Hits Of 1969 (Alshire S-5185) 1969
The Sounds Of Love (A/S-199) 1969
Million Seller Hits Of Today Written By Simon And Garfunkel (Alshire S-5156) 1969
The "Exotic" Sounds Of Love (A/S-201) 1970
Million Seller Hits Arranged And Conducted By Les Baxter (Alshire S-5188) 1970
Que Mango! (Arranged And Conducted By Les Baxter) (Alshire S-5204) 1970
Spectacular Brass! Fantastic Reeds! (Arranged/Conducted By Nelson Riddle) (Alshire S-5229) 1970
Theme From Love Story (Alshire S-5232) 1971
Hit Songs Written By Bacharach And Webb (Audio Spectrum 19) 1972
Carole King Hits (Alshire S-5278) 1972
Americana (Alshire S-5317) 1974
Hits Made Famous By The Beach Boys (Alshire S-5342) 1976
Songs Of The Carpenters (Alshire S-5341) 1976
A Tribute To John Lennon (Alshire S-5380) 1980
Love Songs (CD Alshire ALCD-7) 1986
Plus* Plus* Plus (CD Alshire ALCD-18) 1986
Romantic Songs Of The Sea (CD Alshire ALCD-20) 1986
Nelson Riddle With The 101 Strings (CD Alshire ALCD-27) 1987
Magnificent Digital Sound (CD Alshire ALCD-28) 1987
Tribute To Henry Mancini (CD Alshire ALCD-75) 1989
Astro-Sounds: From Beyond the Year 2000 (CD Caroline/Scamp SCP-9717-2) 1996
Que Mango! Les Baxter with the 101 Strings (CD Caroline/Scamp SCP-9718-2) 1996
Instrumental Favorites: The 101 Strings, Featuring The Soul Of Spain (CD Time Life Music R986-21) 1996

Strings For Lovers (CD Alshire ALCD-5221) [Box] 1996
Simply Beautiful Music (CD Madacy 7327) [Box] 1996

Cascading Strings

Cascading Strings were led by John Gregory. He was an arranger and film composer. He made more than 2,000 records, from covers to easy listening to Latin American music. In terms of easy listening, he was an imitator and, therefore, an 'also ran', recording mostly for Phillips. His arrangements are excellent if a little lack-lustre and well worth listening to. His musical hero must surely have been Mantovani.

Serenade In Blue (Contour Stereo 6870 604) 1960
Cascading Strings (Wing Records WL 1028, 680 922 TL) 1960
Golden Memories (Philips 6308 061) 1971
Spotlight On The Cascading Strings (Philips 6625 0200) 1972

Tommy Garrett

(1939-2015, American)

Tommy 'Snuff' Garrett was an A&R man and record producer active in the 1950s, 1960s and 1970s. He obviously spotted a gap in the market for easy listening guitar music, though without the 'beat', and dived into it. If you like The Shadows and you like easy listening, you will love the 50 Guitars series. He covers songs from all around the world and is irrepressibly the romantic fantasist, which makes these albums perfect for lovers to swoon to. I love them!

50 Guitars Go South Of The Border (Liberty LBY 1011, LMM 13005) 1962
50 Guitars Visit Hawaii (Liberty SLBY 1108) 1962
50 Guitars Go Country (Liberty LMM-13025) US 1962
Return To Paradise (Liberty SLBY 1289) 1965
Love Songs From South Of The Border (Liberty SLBY 1302) 1966
The 50 Guitars In Love (Liberty LBS 83031) 1967
Our Love Affair (Liberty LBL 83096) 1968
Romantic Sounds Of 50 Guitars Of... (Sunset Records SLS 50288 Stereo) 1968
50 Guitars For Midnight Lovers (Liberty LBS 83416) 1970
Garrett also put together a regular easy listening orchestra, whose recorded output is every bit as worthy as his 50 Guitars outfit. See below:

Midnight String Quartet:
Rhapsodies For Young Lovers (Viva VS-6001) 1966
Spanish Rhapsodies For Young Lovers (Viva V-36004) 1967
Rhapsodies For Young Lovers, Vol. Two (Viva V-36008) 1967
Love Rhapsodies (Viva V-36013) 1967
The Look Of Love (Viva V-36015) 1968
Goodnight My Love (Viva V-36019) 1968

Rhapsodies For Young Lovers, Vol. Three (Viva V-36022) 1969
Chamber Music For Lovers (Viva V-36024) 1969

Midnight Strings Orchestra:
Reunited (Excelsior XRP 7011) 1980
Reminiscing (with Syd Dale) (Excelsior XRP 7012) 1980
Evergreen (Excelsior XRP 7017) 1981
On The Radio (Excelsior XRP 7015) 1981
Ride Like The Wind (Excelsior XRP 7016) 1981

Horst Jankowski featuring the Jankowski Singers

(1936-1998, German)

Horst Janowski is one of our one-hit wonders, being remembered for his 1965 wonderful easy listening singles chart smash hit 'A Walk in the Black Forest'. He was essentially a jazz pianist, as well as a composer, arranger and band leader, who struck gold with this easy listening classic.

A Walk In The Black Forest (Philips PE20) 1965
Enjoy (Fontana Special SFL 13074 701 826 WPY) 1968
The Black Forest Crystal Clear Piano – So What's New (Mercury Monaural MG 21093) Undated, probably 1960s

The Hollyridge Strings

Arranged and conducted by Stu Phillips (1929-)

Stu Phillips is a renowned American composer, conductor and producer known for his work in film and television. He has had a prolific career spanning decades, with notable contributions to the music of popular TV shows like *The Monkees* and *Knight Rider*. Phillips' talent extends to various genres, showcasing his versatility in the industry.

The Hollyridge Strings (and their offshoots: Hollyridge Strings, Holyridge Strings, Las Cuerdas De Hollyridge, Stu Phillips & The Hollyridge Strings, The Hollyridge Strings And Chorus, The Hollyridge Strings Orchestra) is a musical ensemble that gained recognition for their easy listening and instrumental covers of popular songs. Their albums, featuring lush string arrangements, have been well-received by music lovers, making them a notable name in the world of beautiful and soothing instrumental music. He had an obvious love for the music of The Beatles!

The Beach Boys Songbook: Romantic Instrumentals By The Hollyridge Strings (Capitol Records ST 2156) 1964
The Beatles Song Book (Capitol Records ST2116) 1964
The Beatles Song Book-Vol 2 (Capitol Records ST 2202) 1964
Play Hit Songs Made Famous By Elvis Presley (Capitol Records T22221) 1964
The Hollyridge Strings Play Hits Made Famous By The Four Seasons

(Capitol Records ST2119) 1964
Christmas Favorites (Capitol Records T2404) 1965
The Nat King Cole Song Book (Capitol Records ST2310) 1965
The New Beatles Song Book (Capitol Records T2429) 1966
Oldies But Goldies (Capitol Records T2464) 1966
The Beatles Songbook Vol. 4 (Capitol Records ST2656) 1967
Play The Beach Boys Songbook – Vol. 2 (Capitol Records ST2749) 1967
Play The Hits Of Simon & Garfunkel (Capitol Records ST 2998) 1968
The Beatles Song Book Vol. 5 (Capitol Records T2876) 1968
The Beatles Song Book (Capitol Records ST 2876) 1968
The Hollyridge Strings, The Hollywood Pops Orchestra, Eddie Dunstedter, The Hollywood Bowl Symphony Orchestra – The Wonderful World Of Christmas (2×LP, Compilation, Club Edition) (Capitol Records SQBO-91521) 1968
The George, John, Paul & Ringo Songbook (Capitol Records ST839) 1971
Hits Of The 70s (Capitol Records ST883) 1972
Norwegian Wood (CD, Compilation, Stereo) (Capitol Records TOCP-7572) 1993

Pepi Jaramillo And His Latin American Rhythm
(1921-2001, Mexican)
Pepe Jaramillo played smooth piano in nightclubs. Starting in Mexico, he travelled to London and started to record with EMI in the 1960s and 1970s. Very much an 'also-ran', he, nevertheless, created the sweetest of diner background music, which will have provided a backdrop to dinner parties everywhere.

His pop cover versions were run through with Latin rhythms, giving them the kind of romantic flavour that easy listening demands.

The Romantic World of Pepe Jaramillo (Capitol Records ST 6136) 1965
Mexico Champagne (EMI Columbia Studio 2 Stereo TWO 255) 1969
Moonlight In Mexico (EMI COLUMBIA Studio 2 Stereo TWO 192) 1968
Pepe ON The Continent (EMI COLUMBIA Studio 2 Stereo TWO 122) 1968
Just For You (One-Up, One-Up OU 2224, 0C 054-06 895) 1979

Knightsbridge Strings
Graham Strange, mentioned in the Acknowledgements above, introduced me to this easy listening 'brand'. All I have been able to find out about them is that they were England's answer to 101 Strings. There will have been some music business mogul, the Simon Cowell of the day, who will have twigged there was money to be made packaging easy listening music for the UK and its dominions and colonies, but I have not been able to find out who. The name was used for releases on both the UK label Top Rank and Nashville-based Monument Records. The 'brand' used various names for its orchestral easy listening line-ups, such as The Knightsbridge Strings, The Knightsbridge Singing Strings and The Knightsbridge Strings & Voices. An 'also-ran' indeed,

there is nothing here to blow your socks off, but it is all delightful stuff (pop covers and romantic moods predominating), and done in the best possible easy listening taste, as Kenny Everett might have said, and I am very glad to have come across it in Graham's wide-ranging vinyl collections.

A String Of Pearls (Top Rank, Top Rank International 35/031) 1959
The Strings Sway (Top Rank International BUY 017) 1960
Blue Violins (Top Rank International BUY 015) 1960
Latin Cameos (Top Rank International RS 615) US 1960
The Knightsbridge Strings Go Pop (Monument MAS 13003, MAM 13003) US 1966
¾ Time (Monument Artistry Series MAS 13001) 1966
Boots Randolph With The Knightsbridge Strings & Voices (Monument LMO 5012) 1968
Love Story (Music From The Paramount Picture) (Boulevard 4052) 1971
Immortal Melodies (CD, Album) (Hallmark Music & Entertainment 709892) 2010

Francis Lai
(1932-1970, French)
Already mentioned above in the 'Overview', Francis Lai enchanted audiences with his emotive melodies. Known for his evocative film scores, Lai's music captured the essence of romance and nostalgia. Hits like 'Love Story' and 'A Man And A Woman' remain classics, showcasing his ability to tug at heartstrings through lush orchestration. His work endures as a testament to the power of musical storytelling.

The Best Of Francis Lai (From the Original Motion Picture Soundtracks of 'A Man and a Woman' and 'Live for Life') (United Artists UAS 6656) 1968
Love Story (MCA 27017) 1971
More Love Themes (Kapp) (KS-3646) 1971
Plays Francis Lai (UA UAS 5515) 1971
French Themes (United Artists UAS 5360) 1972
Francis Lai And His Orchestra Play The Compositions Of Burt Bacharach, Gato Barbieri, John Barry… (United Artists UA-LA095-F) 1973
Love In The Rain (The Man And His Music) (Audiofidelity AFE 6301 LP) 1981
Bilitis (Original Soundtrack) (CD Melodie Editions-23 80035-2) [French Import] 1987
The Very Best Of Francis Lai (CD Skyline SLCD 817) [Swedish Import] 1990
A Man And A Woman/Live For Life (CD DRG 12612) 1996

Eddie Calvert
(1922-1978, English)
Eddie Calvert, the master of the trumpet, enchanted listeners with his smooth and soothing melodies, epitomising easy listening music. His chart-topping

hit 'Oh Mein Papa' remains an iconic classic, showcasing his remarkable talent and unforgettable contribution to the world of music.

The Man With The Golden Trumpet (Columbia 335 1020) 1954
Eddie's Golden Song Book (Columbia 33SX 1385) 1962

Ennio Morricone
(1928-2020, Italian)
Already mentioned in the 'Overview' above, Ennio Morricone wove cinematic magic through his evocative compositions. His scores, notably for spaghetti westerns and iconic films like *The Good, The Bad And The Ugly*, resonated with timeless emotion.

Morricone's ability to create dramatic, atmospheric soundscapes, which lend themselves readily to easy listening reinterpretation, made him a legendary figure in the music of our golden age.

Once Upon A Time In The West (LSP-4736) 1972
A Fistful Of Dollars (RCA Victor RD-7875) 1967
Teorema (VMLP188) 1968
The Good, The Bad And The Ugly (Eureka EPL 2890(S)) 1966

The Mystic Moods Orchestra
Mentioned in the 'Overview' above, The Mystic Moods Orchestra, despite their undeniably innovative musical talent, faced challenges in achieving widespread success in the easy listening genre. In an era dominated by established artists and orchestras, breaking through proved difficult. Additionally, their experimental and unconventional approach to instrumentation and arrangements sometimes puzzled traditional listeners.

Though they created beguiling, lush soundscapes, these did not achieve the wide appeal of more mainstream artists. Marketing and visibility issues also hindered their rise to stardom. Nonetheless, their ingenious, one might say, avant-garde sound continues to be influential in modern easy listening and new-age music.

One Stormy Night (PHS-600-205) 1966
Nighttide (PHS-600-213) 1966
More Than Music (PHS-600-231) 1967
Mexico! (Also Titled: Mexican Trip) (PHS-600-250) 1967
The Mystic Moods Of Love (PHS-200-260) 1968
Emotions (PHS-200-277) 1968
Extensions (PHS-200-301) 1969
Love Token (PHS-200-321) 1970
Stormy Weekend (PHS-200-342) 1970
English Muffins (PHS-200-349) 1970

CD titles re-released on Cema and Capitol's 'Right Stuff' Label in 'Colossus' Digital Stereo:

Mystic Moods Country (CD Cema Special Products 521-56928) 1993
One Stormy Night (T2-66685) 1993
Highway One (T2-32048) 1995
Nighttide (T2-66687) 1995
Moods For A Stormy Night (T2-66686) 1995
Stormy Weekend (T2-66695) 1995
More Than Music (T2-32045) 1995
Emotions (T2-32047) 1995
Stormy Memories (Featuring Rene Hamaty on piano) (T2-66697) 1995

Norrie Paramor

(1914-1979, English)

Paramor was a man of many musical talents who led several orchestras, not least of all the BBC Midland Radio Orchestra, most famously scoring the theme tune to TV's first gritty police drama series *Z Cars*. He scored film soundtracks, most notably for the film *Doctor In Distress*. He produced records for artists, including Cliff Richard and The Shadows. While most of his output might be best described as strictly 'mood' music, he did try his hand, not always convincingly – as he himself admitted in a late 1950s *Melody Maker* interview, it should be added – at easy listening. Still, his albums sold well and made for more than pleasant background music, particularly on the album *Autumn*, which features the haunting wordless vocals, ala Ray Conniff, of Patricia Clark.

In London, In Love (Capitol ST-10025) 1956
London After Dark (Capitol ST-10052) 1957
The Zodiac Suite (Capitol ST-10073) 1957
Moods (Capitol ST-10130) 1958
Jet Flight (Capitol ST-10190) 1959
Autumn (With The 'Moody, In-And-Out Voice' Of Patricia Clark) (Capitol ST-10212) 1960
Amor, Amor! (Capitol ST-10238) 1961
Strings! Staged For Sound (Capitol ST-1639) 1962
In London…In Love Again (With The 'Floating Voice' Of Patricia Clark) (Capitol ST-2071) 1963
Warm And Willing (With The 'Spun-Gold Voice' Of Patricia Clark) (Capitol ST-2357) 1964
In Tokyo, In Love (Capitol ST-2526) 1964
Soul Coaxing (Studio 2 Two 207) [UK Import] 1968
Love At First Sight (Polydor 184358) 1969
Silver Serenade (BBC REB 272) [UK Import] 1977
BBC Radio Top Tunes (CD Emporio EMPRCD-660)
In London. In Love/Autumn (CD Collectors' Choice)

Nelson Riddle

(1921-1985, American)

Nelson Riddle's claim to fame lies with the wonderful work he did with the great vocalists of the day, not least of all Frank Sinatra, when he arrived at Capitol Records. He was in much demand thereafter as an arranger, but he did find time to make several solo albums of his own, some of which fit very nicely into the easy listening mode. He did cover versions of pop songs, but for me, they are rather too up-tempo to qualify as truly easy listening. However, his 1958 *Sea Of Dreams* album, while being original work and lacking the familiarity of pop songs – which some may argue is the real appeal of the best of easy listening music – nevertheless transports one off into a world of fantasy and sensuality, another of the essential attributes of easy listening orchestral music. The cover of *Sea Of Dreams* also ticks all the boxes of easy listening graphics and design: there is a naked woman whose lower half is wrapped in what looks like lilac chiffon. The sea is her home, her hair sways with a gentle current and a spray of white flowers lights up her enchanting pearl-white smile and sensuous red lips.

Tender Touch (Capitol T-753) 1957
Sea Of Dreams (Capitol T-915) 1958
The Joy Of Living (Capitol ST-1148) 1959
Love Tide (Capitol ST-1571) 1961
Love Is A Game Of Poker (Capitol ST-1817) 1962
More Hit Tv Themes (Capitol ST-1869) 1963
White On White, Shangri-La, Charade, And Other Hits Of 1964 (Reprise RS-6120) 1964
The Bright And The Beautiful (Liberty LST-7508) 1967
The Riddle Of Today (Liberty LST-7532) 1968

David Rose

(1910-1990, England born, raised from the age of four in the USA)

Having once heard it, who could ever forget the gorgeous sauciness of David Rose's 1962 burlesque composition and performance of 'The Stripper'? Hardly easy listening, but boy o boy, can one not transport oneself off to the sleaziest stripper joint in town? Whatever else it does, there was a lot more to David Rose than 'that'. He wrote prolifically for radio, TV and film, most memorably the theme tune to US TV western series *Bonanza*, and won numerous Emmys and Grammys as well as receiving an Oscar nomination. His music leans more to light classical than pop and he didn't do pop covers, but when he wanted to be romantic, he composed what can plausibly be described as easy listening. This makes him very much a very worthy 'also ran'. And it should not be forgotten that the Muzak Corporation liked his orchestrally zany record *Holiday For Strings* so much that they commissioned him to do a 'wallpaper' version of it for their use.

Beautiful Music To Love By (MGM E-3067) 1953
Nostalgia (MGM E-3134) 1954
Lover's Serenade (MGM E-3289) 1955
Autumn Leaves (MGM SE-3592) 1957
Secret Songs For Young Lovers (with Andre Previn) (MGM SE-3716) 1958
David Rose Plays David Rose (MGM SE-3811) 1959
Spectacular Strings (MGM SE-3895) 1961
Cimarron And Other Great Themes (MGM SE-3953) 1961
Bonanza (MGM SE-3960) 1961
The Stripper And Other Fun Songs For The Family (MGM Records SE-4062)
The Very Best Of David Rose (MGM SE-4155) 1962
The Velvet Beat (MGM SE-4307) 1965
In A Mellow Mood (Masterseal ST-9000)
Themes From The Great Screen Epics (Capitol ST-2627) 1967
Happy Heart (Capitol ST-393) 1969

Sandpipers

In the sunlit soundscape of the late 1960s and 1970s, The Sandpipers emerged as gentle troubadours of easy listening elegance. With honeyed harmonies and a penchant for embracing timeless melodies, they crafted sonic landscapes as serene as a calm ocean at dawn. Songs like 'Guantanamera' and 'Come Saturday Morning' create moods of tranquil escapism, transporting listeners to a world of blissful reverie. They are as much a part of our golden age of easy listening as anyone.

Guantanamera (A&M Mayfair AMLB 1004) 1970

Sounds Orchestral

Sounds Orchestral, a notable easy listening group of the 1960s, specialised in crafting smooth, instrumental arrangements that resonated with a wide audience. Led by John Schroeder, their rendition of 'Cast Your Fate To The Wind' became an iconic hit. Their instrumental prowess, enriched by keyboards and strings, delivered a mellow, soothing sound that was perfect for relaxation. Sounds Orchestra's music, accessible and sophisticated, fits easily into the canon of easy listening.

Cast Your Fate To The Wind (Piccadilly NPL 38014 Monaural)

Sounds Incorporated

Sounds Incorporated, a saxophone-led instrumental sextet from Dartford, Kent, England, formed in 1961. Their initial success came when they filled in for The Blue Caps during Gene Vincent's UK tour. Their debut single 'Mogambo' was on Parlophone, followed by three singles on Decca, the last being 'Keep Movin'', produced by Joe Meek. They were known for their use of the unique 'Clavioline' keyboard. In 1963, they caught The Beatles' attention in Hamburg and were signed to NEMS by Brian Epstein, touring as the opening act, even at the famous Shea Stadium concert. They released singles on Columbia, with 'William Tell' reaching number two in the Australian charts in 1964. After several albums and a transition to Sounds Inc in 1967, the group disbanded in 1971, following individual pursuits.

Sounds Incorporated (Columbia TA-33SX 1659) 1964
Sounds Incorporated (Columbia Studio 2 Stereo TWO 144) 1964
Sounds Incorporated (Metronome HLP 10 282) (Germany) 1970
Maxwell's Silver Hammer (Calendar Records SR66-9811) (Australia) 1972

Waikiki Islanders

The Waikiki Islanders, led by Danny Stewart, were easy listening masters, crafting Hawaiian melodies with ukuleles, steel guitars and vocal choruses. Their music whisks listeners away to a tranquil island paradise. Their harmoniously exotic tunes paint a serene picture that immerses listeners in a world of sun-drenched calm and beauty.

Hawaiian Magic (Tiffany Records TR-2006) 1960
Shades Of Hawaii (Columbia TWO 177) 1967
Hawaiian Nights (Columbia, Studio 2 Stereo TWO 218) 1968
Hawaiian Honeymoon (Columbia TWO 290, 1E 062 04319) 1970

Roger Williams

(1924-2011, American)
Pianist Roger Williams and his Orchestra specialised in crafting soothing and melodic tunes. Williams' elegant piano work, combined with lush orchestrations, defined their sound. Of their many pop covers hits, tunes like 'Autumn Leaves' and 'Born Free' remain timeless.
Roger Williams Autumn Leaves (KL-1012) 1956
Daydreams (KL-1031) 1956
Songs Of The Fabulous Fifties (KXL-5000) [2] 1957
Almost Paradise (KL-1063) 1957
Till (KL-1081) 1958
Near You (KL-1112) 1959
Always (KS-3056) 1960
Temptation (KS-3217) 1961
Yellow Bird (KS-3244) 1961
Maria (KS-3266) 1962
For You (KS-3336) 1963
Academy Award Winners (KS-3406) 1964
Plays The Hits (KS-3414) 1965
Summer Wind (KS-3434) 1965

I'll Remember You (KS-3470) 1966
Born Free (KS-3501) 1966
Roger! (KS-3512) 1967
More Than A Miracle (KS-3550) 1968
Only For Lovers (KS-3565) 1969
Happy Heart (KS-3595) 1969
Love Theme From 'Romeo And Juliet' (KS-3610) 1969
Love Story (KS-3645) 1971
Summer Of '42 (KS-3650) 1971
Love Theme From 'The Godfather' (KS-3663) 1972"
Play Me (KS-3671) 1972
Ivory Impact (Bainbridge BT-8002) [2] 1982
The Best Of The Beautiful (CD MCA MCAD-5571) 1989
The Greatest Popular Pianist/The Artist's Choice (CD MCA MCAD2-10698) [2] 1992
Instrumental Favorites (CD Time Life Music R-986-06) 1995
Roger Williams Collection (CD Varese Vintage VSD-5908) 1998
Softly As I Leave You (CD Varese Vintage CSD-5984) 1998

The Tequila Brass

The Tequila Brass, a vibrant London-based band of the 1970s, left an indelible mark on the music scene. With their fusion of Latin, jazz, and funk influences, they brought a unique sound to the era.

Led by talented horn players and a charismatic vocalist, the band's energetic performances became a hallmark of their career. Their eponymous album *Tequila Brass*, released in 1973, showcased their musical prowess.

A Taste Of Tijuana (Saga Eros – ERO 8045) 1967
Tamla Meets Tijuana (Music For Pleasure MFP 1381) 1971

Compilations

Easy listening compilations are available worldwide. They cater to diverse tastes, from instrumental tunes to vocal classics. These collections transcend borders, providing a global soundtrack for relaxation and enjoyment, making them accessible to a broad audience. A smattering of examples is given below. Where a country is not specifically mentioned, the albums were released either in the UK or US.

Gimme, Gimmé, Gimme... (AMIGA – 8 55 771)(GDR) 1980
Arne Oit – Arne Oit 50. Valik Estraadilaule (Мелодия – С60-12097-8) (USSR) 1980
Golden Memories (Merco MCO 0016/7/8) 1980
Latin Standard Best (RCA – RJL-2589) (Japan) 1982
Various – 50 Of The Most Loved Records Of Your Life Cassette No. 2 (CBS Special Products T 17692) 1984
1945-1980 Sentimental Journey (Circle Records LP-3900-4) 1980
Quiet Music For Quiet Listening (Reader's Digest BA021) 1986
International Graffiti 3 (Polydor – 819 992-1) (Italy 1988)
The Day War Broke Out (EMI – TC EM 1341) 1989
Test Card Classics: The Girl, The Doll, The Music (Flyback FBDC-2000) 1996
It's Easy Volume 1: High Life (Flyback CHA 2000) 1997
Serenade In The Night (Music & Memories MMD 1091/1)1999
Sentimental Journey (Music & Memories MMD 1019-4-5) 1994
Mood, 20 Original Big Band Hits (JTD 102401 AAD) 1994
The Swingin' Sound of Easy Listening (Reader's Digest RCD6101-5) 2008
Pure Clarinet (SignCD2516) 2006
Biggest Instrumental Hits of the 50s (M&M 2010
Music By Moonlight, 60 Instrumental Easy Listening Favourites (One Day Music DAY3CD069) 2015
Light & Easy (Duet Music ST42) Undated
Sleepy Shores (MFP MFP 50495 Stereo)
Easy Listening Beatles Song Book (Embassy Stereo EMB 31101) 1973
Nice 'n' Easy (Philips 66 053) 1967
Nice 'n' Easy Volume 2 (Philips 6641 076) 1971

Conclusion

Tempora mutantur, nos et mutamur in illis: the times change, and we change with them.

In writing this history, I have focused on the personalities who invented the genre. Without these musical geniuses, their record company executives and A&R men, not to mention entrepreneurs like Jackie Gleason and music moguls like David L. Miller, easy listening music could not have existed. Each one of them, in their various years and decades, brought to the genre something new and compelling. It is obvious from chart entries and album sales, not just in the US and the UK, but around the world, that in its day, orchestral and instrumental easy listening music was immensely popular with an adult generation reeling in a world that was just recovering from a shattering global economic depression and a protracted world war. It was one which was also bewildered, too, by the mid-century rise of rock 'n' roll, a musical genre that, to them, was racially hybrid and distinctly morally unsettling. Added to this was the Cold War with Soviet Russia, with its threat of nuclear annihilation. As crazy as their children were about Elvis, they just couldn't see the appeal musically. No, they didn't want their nerves jangled, they wanted escapism. And they wanted the beautiful things in life, particularly a happy family home life and the romantic love it was built upon. Easy-listening music gave them this.

What is also interesting is how so many countries around the world produced their own easy listening giants. Britain, as discussed, played no small part. In this study, I have given as wide a range of these countries as possible from available research sources.

Easy listening music remained popular throughout the late 1950s, 1960s and 1970s. The Muzak corporation did try to steal easy listening's thunder from the record companies, but they simply didn't have the genius for it. They did start producing copies of pop standards, but they were as dull as ditch water. But that's how things changed: they started playing the originals. Where once you heard Muzak's 'wallpaper' music, in most places now you hear the actual pop standards and contemporary hits being played. Many shopping chains even have their own radio stations playing in the background. Easy listening music somehow got lost in the mix, added to which the adult generation that loved it simply died, while the new generation hardly sees the point of it.

Where younger people did want to hear something playing quietly in the background, they turned to lounge music. In the 1980s and 1990s, there was a revival of what might be called, not exactly 'mood' music, but more simply, 'cool'. If anything pleases or interests nowadays, it is met with the word 'cool'. The lounge revival turned onto the jazz greats, strangely enough, often of their parent's generation, either vocal or instrumental, but not easy listening music. Perhaps it's too big a sound. Maybe it's not for a generation whose 'chic' is of their own peculiar making. If they were reacting to dishevelled grunge music and its fashions, it was not the singular dichotomy their parents faced with the arrival of rock 'n' roll and the youth culture it spawned. The new generation did not fear the world going to hell in a handcart. For them, it either already had, cf. all the various 'extinction' protest groups, or they don't really notice or care that much. They work hard to get affluent and only want to 'chill out' at the end of the day. What they listen to in bars and restaurants is a pleasant mix of jazz, blues and even Latin, with some electronic and House thrown in. Lounge can be sensual, if not exactly romantic; easy listening music, if it was for anything, was all for romance. For the modern generation, romance is considered corny, as corny as, say, Nashville's cross-over country music, easy listening's bedfellow.

And yet, if you go to the streaming services, you will find that the classic easy listening tracks are being downloaded millions and hundreds of thousands of times. On Spotify, Percy Faith's arrangement of 'I Will Follow Him' has, at the time of writing, been played 2,482,778 times! I wonder if the album this track came from sold as many copies. Paul Weston's track, 'I'm Thru With Love', from his seminal *Music For Dreaming* album, has been downloaded 31,547 times. 'Alone Together' from Jackie Gleason's iconic album, *Music For Lovers Only*, has been played 1,710,551 times. While Henri Mancini's own arrangement of 'Moon River' has been played a staggering 14,080,003 times. And what about Mantovani? 'The Theme From Moulin Rouge' from his classic album, *Waltz Encore*, has been played an equally staggering 542,094 times. And this is just on Spotify. On Apple, Deezer and so on, the same story is told. On YouTube, Bert Kaempfert's 'Wonderland By Night' has been viewed 3,069,993 times to date, whilst Percy Faith's 'Theme From a Summer Place', an unbelievable 33,179,000 times. So, I think it's safe to say there are people all over the world who still want to hear orchestral easy listening music.

And, of course, James Last's phenomenal popularity around the world from our golden age right up until his death in 2015 is not to be forgotten. His signature arrangement of 'Orange Blossom Special' has been viewed 21,424,398 times on YouTube.

Bibliography

Bach, Bob and Ginger Mercer. *The Life, Times and Song Lyrics of Our Huckleberry Friend*, Lyle Stuart Inc, 1982.
Borgerson, Janet and Jonathon Schroeder. *Design For Hi-Fi Living*, The MIT Press 2018
Dimery, Robert Gen. Ed. *1001 Albums*, Cassell Illustrated, 2018.
Jones, Dylan. *Ultra Lounge: The Lexicon of Easy Listening*, Universe Publishing, 1997, Martini Music and Easy Listening.
Knopper, Steve, Editor. *Lounge, The Essential Album Guide to Martini Music and Easy Listening*, Visible Ink, 1998.
Lanza, Joseph. *Easy Listening Acid Trip*, Feral House, 2020.
Lanza, Joseph. *Elevator Music*, University Press of Michigan, 2004.
Last, James. *My Autobiography*, Metro, 2007.
Mancini, Henry and Gene Lees. *The Autobiography of Henry Mancini, Did They Mention the Music?*, Cooper Square Press, 2001.
Malone, Bill C. *Country Music USA*, University Of Texas Press, 1993.
Roach, Martin. *Hit Albums*, Virgin Books, 2009.
Scowcroft, Philip L. *British Light Music*, Dance Books, 2013.
Self, Geoffrey. *Light Music in Britain Since 1870*, Ashgate 2001
Weston, Paul and Jo Stafford. *Song Of The Road*, BearManor Media, 2012.

Billboard Books

Number One Adult Contemporary Hits, Wesley Hyatt, 1999
The Adult Songs 1961-2006, 2007.
Top 40 Albums Since 1955, Omnibus Press 1991
Pop Hits 1940-1954, Record Research Inc. 1994.
Hit Singles, Top 20 Charts From 1954 To The Present Day, Backbeat Books 2004

Other Sources

I'd particularly like to thank Graham Sage of 'Recollect Vinyl & CD Fairs' for sourcing difficult-to-find vinyl albums and CDs.
There are various internet radio stations, including orchestra and instrumental easy listening music in their broadcasts, but by far the best is Radio Caprice – easy listening stream. It is dauntingly comprehensive in range.

Misty - The Music of Johnny Mathis

Foreword by Johnny Mathis

Jakob Baekgaard
Foreword by Johnny Mathis
Paperback
192 pages
60 colour photographs
978-1-78951-247-1
£17.99
$24.95

The musical life of this famed jazz/soul singer.

Few singers have been able to change with the times like Johnny Mathis. Although his fame rests on his massive popularity in the 50s and 60s when he competed with Elvis and Frank Sinatra and outsold almost anyone, Mathis has remained relevant through the decades and no other crooner is as technically skilled or able to cover multiple genres so convincingly. Jazz, soul, disco, country, classic and contemporary pop, Mathis has adapted his impressive vocal range to all kinds of music and transgressed the stereotype of what a male voice is supposed to sound like.

The longest-running artist on Columbia, he has been recognized by the record industry with The Recording Academy Lifetime Achievement Award and three recordings in the Grammy Hall of Fame, but so far, there hasn't been an exhaustive examination of his complete recordings in book form. Authorized by Mathis and including fresh insights from himself as well as his producers and arrangers, Misty: The Music of Johnny Mathis, rights that wrong. With detailed discussions of the records and a discography, the book traces Mathis's musical journey from the past to the present and includes a wealth of photos and album scans from his own archive. It's the ideal companion for fans and new listeners interested in exploring one of the most prominent voices in American music.

On Track series

Allman Brothers Band – Andrew Wild 978-1-78952-252-5
Tori Amos – Lisa Torem 978-1-78952-142-9
Aphex Twin – Beau Waddell 978-1-78952-267-9
Asia – Peter Braidis 978-1-78952-099-6
Badfinger – Robert Day-Webb 978-1-878952-176-4
Barclay James Harvest – Keith and Monica Domone 978-1-78952-067-5
Beck – Arthur Lizie 978-1-78952-258-7
The Beatles – Andrew Wild 978-1-78952-009-5
The Beatles Solo 1969-1980 – Andrew Wild 978-1-78952-030-9
Blue Oyster Cult – Jacob Holm-Lupo 978-1-78952-007-1
Blur – Matt Bishop 978-178952-164-1
Marc Bolan and T.Rex – Peter Gallagher 978-1-78952-124-5
Kate Bush – Bill Thomas 978-1-78952-097-2
Camel – Hamish Kuzminski 978-1-78952-040-8
Captain Beefheart – Opher Goodwin 978-1-78952-235-8
Caravan – Andy Boot 978-1-78952-127-6
Cardiacs – Eric Benac 978-1-78952-131-3
Nick Cave and The Bad Seeds – Dominic Sanderson 978-1-78952-240-2
Eric Clapton Solo – Andrew Wild 978-1-78952-141-2
The Clash – Nick Assirati 978-1-78952-077-4
Elvis Costello and The Attractions – Georg Purvis 978-1-78952-129-0
Crosby, Stills and Nash – Andrew Wild 978-1-78952-039-2
Creedence Clearwater Revival – Tony Thompson 978-178952-237-2
The Damned – Morgan Brown 978-1-78952-136-8
Deep Purple and Rainbow 1968-79 – Steve Pilkington 978-1-78952-002-6
Dire Straits – Andrew Wild 978-1-78952-044-6
The Doors – Tony Thompson 978-1-78952-137-5
Dream Theater – Jordan Blum 978-1-78952-050-7
Eagles – John Van der Kiste 978-1-78952-260-0
Earth, Wind and Fire – Bud Wilkins 978-1-78952-272-3
Electric Light Orchestra – Barry Delve 978-1-78952-152-8
Emerson Lake and Palmer – Mike Goode 978-1-78952-000-2
Fairport Convention – Kevan Furbank 978-1-78952-051-4
Peter Gabriel – Graeme Scarfe 978-1-78952-138-2
Genesis – Stuart MacFarlane 978-1-78952-005-7
Gentle Giant – Gary Steel 978-1-78952-058-3
Gong – Kevan Furbank 978-1-78952-082-8
Green Day – William E. Spevack 978-1-78952-261-7
Hall and Oates – Ian Abrahams 978-1-78952-167-2
Hawkwind – Duncan Harris 978-1-78952-052-1
Peter Hammill – Richard Rees Jones 978-1-78952-163-4
Roy Harper – Opher Goodwin 978-1-78952-130-6

Also available from Sonicbond ...

Jimi Hendrix – Emma Stott 978-1-78952-175-7
The Hollies – Andrew Darlington 978-1-78952-159-7
Horslips – Richard James 978-1-78952-263-1
The Human League and The Sheffield Scene –
Andrew Darlington 978-1-78952-186-3
The Incredible String Band – Tim Moon 978-1-78952-107-8
Iron Maiden – Steve Pilkington 978-1-78952-061-3
Joe Jackson – Richard James 978-1-78952-189-4
Jefferson Airplane – Richard Butterworth 978-1-78952-143-6
Jethro Tull – Jordan Blum 978-1-78952-016-3
Elton John in the 1970s – Peter Kearns 978-1-78952-034-7
Billy Joel – Lisa Torem 978-1-78952-183-2
Judas Priest – John Tucker 978-1-78952-018-7
Kansas – Kevin Cummings 978-1-78952-057-6
The Kinks – Martin Hutchinson 978-1-78952-172-6
Korn – Matt Karpe 978-1-78952-153-5
Led Zeppelin – Steve Pilkington 978-1-78952-151-1
Level 42 – Matt Philips 978-1-78952-102-3
Little Feat – Georg Purvis - 978-1-78952-168-9
Aimee Mann – Jez Rowden 978-1-78952-036-1
Joni Mitchell – Peter Kearns 978-1-78952-081-1
The Moody Blues – Geoffrey Feakes 978-1-78952-042-2
Motorhead – Duncan Harris 978-1-78952-173-3
Nektar – Scott Meze – 978-1-78952-257-0
New Order – Dennis Remmer – 978-1-78952-249-5
Nightwish – Simon McMurdo – 978-1-78952-270-9
Laura Nyro – Philip Ward 978-1-78952-182-5
Mike Oldfield – Ryan Yard 978-1-78952-060-6
Opeth – Jordan Blum 978-1-78-952-166-5
Pearl Jam – Ben L. Connor 978-1-78952-188-7
Tom Petty – Richard James 978-1-78952-128-3
Pink Floyd – Richard Butterworth 978-1-78952-242-6
The Police – Pete Braidis 978-1-78952-158-0
Porcupine Tree – Nick Holmes 978-1-78952-144-3
Queen – Andrew Wild 978-1-78952-003-3
Radiohead – William Allen 978-1-78952-149-8
Rancid – Paul Matts 989-1-78952-187-0
Renaissance – David Detmer 978-1-78952-062-0
REO Speedwagon – Jim Romag 978-1-78952-262-4
The Rolling Stones 1963-80 – Steve Pilkington 978-1-78952-017-0
The Smiths and Morrissey – Tommy Gunnarsson 978-1-78952-140-5
Spirit – Rev. Keith A. Gordon – 978-1-78952- 248-8
Stackridge – Alan Draper 978-1-78952-232-7

Status Quo the Frantic Four Years – Richard James 978-1-78952-160-3
Steely Dan – Jez Rowden 978-1-78952-043-9
Steve Hackett – Geoffrey Feakes 978-1-78952-098-9
Tears For Fears – Paul Clark - 978-178952-238-9
Thin Lizzy – Graeme Stroud 978-1-78952-064-4
Tool – Matt Karpe 978-1-78952-234-1
Toto – Jacob Holm-Lupo 978-1-78952-019-4
U2 – Eoghan Lyng 978-1-78952-078-1
UFO – Richard James 978-1-78952-073-6
Van Der Graaf Generator – Dan Coffey 978-1-78952-031-6
Van Halen – Morgan Brown – 9781-78952-256-3
The Who – Geoffrey Feakes 978-1-78952-076-7
Roy Wood and the Move – James R Turner 978-1-78952-008-8
Yes – Stephen Lambe 978-1-78952-001-9
Frank Zappa 1966 to 1979 – Eric Benac 978-1-78952-033-0
Warren Zevon – Peter Gallagher 978-1-78952-170-2
10CC – Peter Kearns 978-1-78952-054-5

Decades Series

The Bee Gees in the 1960s – Andrew Mon Hughes et al 978-1-78952-148-1
The Bee Gees in the 1970s – Andrew Mon Hughes et al 978-1-78952-179-5
Black Sabbath in the 1970s – Chris Sutton 978-1-78952-171-9
Britpop – Peter Richard Adams and Matt Pooler 978-1-78952-169-6
Phil Collins in the 1980s – Andrew Wild 978-1-78952-185-6
Alice Cooper in the 1970s – Chris Sutton 978-1-78952-104-7
Alice Cooper in the 1980s – Chris Sutton 978-1-78952-259-4
Curved Air in the 1970s – Laura Shenton 978-1-78952-069-9
Donovan in the 1960s – Jeff Fitzgerald 978-1-78952-233-4
Bob Dylan in the 1980s – Don Klees 978-1-78952-157-3
Brian Eno in the 1970s – Gary Parsons 978-1-78952-239-6
Faith No More in the 1990s – Matt Karpe 978-1-78952-250-1
Fleetwood Mac in the 1970s – Andrew Wild 978-1-78952-105-4
Fleetwood Mac in the 1980s – Don Klees 978-178952-254-9
Focus in the 1970s – Stephen Lambe 978-1-78952-079-8
Free and Bad Company in the 1970s – John Van der Kiste 978-1-78952-178-8
Genesis in the 1970s – Bill Thomas 978178952-146-7
George Harrison in the 1970s – Eoghan Lyng 978-1-78952-174-0
Kiss in the 1970s – Peter Gallagher 978-1-78952-246-4
Manfred Mann's Earth Band in the 1970s – John Van der Kiste 978178952-243-3
Marillion in the 1980s – Nathaniel Webb 978-1-78952-065-1
Van Morrison in the 1970s – Peter Childs - 978-1-78952-241-9
Mott the Hoople and Ian Hunter in the 1970s –
John Van der Kiste 978-1-78-952-162-7

Pink Floyd In The 1970s – Georg Purvis 978-1-78952-072-9
Suzi Quatro in the 1970s – Darren Johnson 978-1-78952-236-5
Queen in the 1970s – James Griffiths 978-1-78952-265-5
Roxy Music in the 1970s – Dave Thompson 978-1-78952-180-1
Slade in the 1970s – Darren Johnson 978-1-78952-268-6
Status Quo in the 1980s – Greg Harper 978-1-78952-244-0
Tangerine Dream in the 1970s – Stephen Palmer 978-1-78952-161-0
The Sweet in the 1970s – Darren Johnson 978-1-78952-139-9
Uriah Heep in the 1970s – Steve Pilkington 978-1-78952-103-0
Van der Graaf Generator in the 1970s – Steve Pilkington 978-1-78952-245-7
Rick Wakeman in the 1970s – Geoffrey Feakes 978-1-78952-264-8
Yes in the 1980s – Stephen Lambe with David Watkinson 978-1-78952-125-2

On Screen series

Carry On... – Stephen Lambe 978-1-78952-004-0
David Cronenberg – Patrick Chapman 978-1-78952-071-2
Doctor Who: The David Tennant Years – Jamie Hailstone 978-1-78952-066-8
James Bond – Andrew Wild 978-1-78952-010-1
Monty Python – Steve Pilkington 978-1-78952-047-7
Seinfeld Seasons 1 to 5 – Stephen Lambe 978-1-78952-012-5

Other Books

1967: A Year In Psychedelic Rock 978-1-78952-155-9
1970: A Year In Rock – John Van der Kiste 978-1-78952-147-4
1973: The Golden Year of Progressive Rock 978-1-78952-165-8
Babysitting A Band On The Rocks – G.D. Praetorius 978-1-78952-106-1
Eric Clapton Sessions – Andrew Wild 978-1-78952-177-1
Derek Taylor: For Your Radioactive Children –
Andrew Darlington 978-1-78952-038-5
The Golden Road: The Recording History of The Grateful Dead – John Kilbride 978-1-78952-156-6
Iggy and The Stooges On Stage 1967-1974 – Per Nilsen 978-1-78952-101-6
Jon Anderson and the Warriors – the road to Yes –
David Watkinson 978-1-78952-059-0
Magic: The David Paton Story – David Paton 978-1-78952-266-2
Misty: The Music of Johnny Mathis – Jakob Baekgaard 978-1-78952-247-1
Nu Metal: A Definitive Guide – Matt Karpe 978-1-78952-063-7
Tommy Bolin: In and Out of Deep Purple – Laura Shenton 978-1-78952-070-5
Maximum Darkness – Deke Leonard 978-1-78952-048-4
The Twang Dynasty – Deke Leonard 978-1-78952-049-1

and many more to come!

Would you like to write for Sonicbond Publishing?

We are mainly a music publisher, but we also occasionally publish in other genres including film and television. At Sonicbond Publishing we are always on the look-out for authors, particularly for our two main series, On Track and Decades.

Mixing fact with in depth analysis, the On Track series examines the entire recorded work of a particular musical artist or group. All genres are considered from easy listening and jazz to 60s soul to 90s pop, via rock and metal.

The Decades series singles out a particular decade in an artist or group's history and focuses on that decade in more detail than may be allowed in the On Track series.

While professional writing experience would, of course, be an advantage, the most important qualification is to have real enthusiasm and knowledge of your subject. First-time authors are welcomed, but the ability to write well in English is essential.

Sonicbond Publishing has distribution throughout Europe and North America, and all our books are also published in E-book form. Authors will be paid a royalty based on sales of their book. Further details about our books are available from www.sonicbondpublishing.com. To contact us, complete the contact form there or email info@sonicbondpublishing.co.uk